Love's Labor's Won

by Scott Kaiser

Muse of Fire Books

© 2017 by Scott Kaiser.

All rights reserved. No part of this publication may be reproduced by any means, electronic, mechanical or otherwise, without written permission of the author.

Permission for public performance of any kind must be secured in advance from the author or his agents in writing, and is subject to payment of a royalty.

Muse of Fire Books
Ashland, OR 97520

ScottKaiserShakespeare.com

Cover image designed by Wall-to-Wall Studios
for the Carnegie Mellon University
School of Drama production.

Author photo: Jenny Graham

Editor: Amy Miller

First printing: 2018

Printed in the United States of America

In loving memory of
Kenneth Washington

INTRODUCTION

> Berowne: Our wooing doth not end like an old play:
> Jack hath not Jill.
>
> *Love's Labor's Lost* 5.2.874

Over thirty years ago, while playing King Ferdinand in a student production, I began to notice that *Love's Labor's Lost* stands out as an odd duck among Shakespeare's comedies.

That's because, as the final curtain comes down, absolutely nothing is resolved. Instead, we're left with a heap of questions: Will the four men—Ferdinand, Dumaine, Longaville, and Berowne—endure the penance required of them by their lovers? Will the four women—the Princess, Katherine, Maria, and Rosaline—take them back after a year as promised? Will their relationships survive adversity and separation? Or will they wither and perish?

Such a strange ending for a comedy! Instead of celebration, like *A Midsummer Night's Dream*, Shakespeare gives us disappointment. Instead of forgiveness, like *Much Ado About Nothing*, he gives us penance. Instead of weddings, like *As You Like It*, he gives us farewells. Instead of eternal union, like *Twelfth Night*, he gives us uncertain separation.

That's when I realized that Shakespeare had crafted the ending of *Love's Labor's Lost* to be a cliffhanger—a vexing non-ending designed to entice you back to the theater to find out what happens next.

And that's why I believe, as many scholars do, that Shakespeare wrote a long-lost play known as *Love's Labor's Won*—a sequel to *Love's Labor's Lost*.

Unfortunately, there are only two tenuous shreds of evidence to support that idea. First, there's a tantalizing reference to a play entitled *Love Labours Wonne* in a 1598 essay by Francis Meres called "Wit's Treasury." And, second, there's an intriguing mention of a play called *Loves Labor Won* in the 1603 inventory of a bookseller named Christopher Hunt. Not much to go on.

Some scholars maintain that Shakespeare's *Much Ado About Nothing* is the sequel to *Love's Labor's Lost*. But that defies common sense, for not a single character from one play appears in the other. The more sensible approach is to ponder: Would the playwright who gave us *Antony and Cleopatra* as a follow-up to *Julius Caesar*, who gave us *Merry Wives* as a spin-off for Falstaff, who gave us a four-part Wars of the Roses and a four-part Henriad, simply abandon the characters of *Love's Labor's Lost* without bringing them back together? I think not.

Three decades later, I decided that I had waited long enough to see the ending. I would have to write the sequel myself. Not by satirizing the Bard, as so many writers do these days, but the way Shakespeare might have written it—using his vocabulary, his metrical wizardry, and his rhetorical flair.

So I imagined the outbreak of a European war that separates our lovers, not for just a year, but for four long years of hardship. I imagined that each of these lovers suffers a terrible loss. I imagined that the crucible of war changes all of them, irrevocably. Then, as the conflict subsides, I imagined, at the signing of a peace treaty, the couples coming together again for a much-delayed reunion.

Here then, is *The Second Part of Love's Labor's Lost*, otherwise known as *Love's Labor's Won*.

—Scott Kaiser

PRODUCTION HISTORY

Love's Labor's Won enjoyed a university production in the Philip Chosky Theater at Carnegie Mellon University in November of 2017. The director was Scott Kaiser; the scenic designer was Fiona Rhodes; the costume designer was Natalie Burton; the lighting designer was Alex Gibson; the sound designer/composer/arranger was Anthony Stultz; the voice and text director was Gary Logan; the music director was Sarah Pickett; the stage manager was Brennan Cole Felbinger.

The cast was as follows:

WAR	Jordan Plutzer
ISABELLE	Kennedy McMann
ROSALINE	Aubyn Heglie
KATHERINE	Myha'la Herrold
MARIA	Eleanor Pearson
JAQUENETTA	Rayquila Durham
FERDINAND	Christopher J. Essex
BEROWNE	Christian Strange
DUMAINE	Chase Del Rey
LONGAVILLE	Kyle Decker
COSTARD	Jordan Plutzer

Love's Labor's Won received a professional premiere production at the Illinois Shakespeare Festival in July of 2015 under the artistic direction of Kevin Rich. The director was Sara Becker; the scenic designer was Jen Kazmierczak; the costume designer was Nicholas Hartman; the lighting designer was Cassie Mings; the Stage Manager was Audra Kuchling.

The cast was as follows:

WAR	Henson Keys
ISABELLE	Leslie Lank
ROSALINE	Quetta Carpenter
KATHERINE	Faith Servant
MARIA	Natalie Blackman
JAQUENETTA	Sara J. Griffin
FERDINAND	Thom Miller
BEROWNE	Steve Wojtas
DUMAINE	Ronald Román
LONGAVILLE	Colin Lawrence
COSTARD	Colin Trevino-Odell

Love's Labor's Won received an academic premiere production at the Lee Center for the Arts at Seattle University in November of 2014. The director was Scott Kaiser; the scenic designer was Carol Wolfe Clay; the costume designer was Harmony Arnold; the lighting designer was Kent Cubbage; the sound designer was Dominic CodyKramers; the music director was Casey James.

The cast was as follows:

WAR	Nick Pineda
ISABELLE	Elizabeth Rathbone
ROSALINE	Meme Garcia
KATHERINE	Gabrielle Sigrist
MARIA	Madison Kylie Spillman
JAQUENETTA	Ariana Chriest
FERDINAND	Michael Notestine
BEROWNE	Jacob Swanson
DUMAINE	Connor Fogarty
LONGAVILLE	Dylan Zucati
COSTARD	Marshall J. Lewis

THE PLAY IN BRIEF

At the end of Shakespeare's comedy *Love's Labor's Lost*, the romantic hopes of four young couples are abruptly dashed by the sudden death of the King of France. Their courting suspended, the lovers vow to meet again after a year has passed. But the death of the French King sparks a European war, delaying their reunion for four turbulent years. The couples meet again in Paris for the negotiation of an armistice. But the crucible of war has changed them all. Will their relationships survive?

CHARACTERS

WAR, *ageless, male*

ISABELLE, *Princess of France*
ROSALINE, *disguised as Emmanuel Lanier, a war journalist*
KATHERINE, *friend to Isabelle*
MARIA, *ambassador of France*
JAQUENETTA, *a war entertainer*

FERDINAND, *King of Navarre*
BEROWNE, *a war entertainer, a captain*
DUMAINE, *a wealthy munitions manufacturer*
LONGAVILLE, *imprisoned in the palace*
COSTARD, *servant to Ferdinand, a corporal*

PRONUNCIATION GUIDE

Berowne = buh-ROON
Costard = KAW-sturd
Jaquenetta = jack-uh-NET-uh
Lanier = luh-NEER
Louis = LOO-iss
Maria = muh-RYE-uh
Navarre = nuh-VAHR
Rosaline = RAW-zuh-line

PRODUCTION NOTES

PERIOD

The play has been successfully set at the time of the signing of the armistice that ended the First World War—November 1918. I strongly recommend this approach. Any other conceptual interpretation must be approved in writing in advance of production.

PLACE

The Royal Palace, Paris.

TIME

The play takes place within a period of exactly 24 hours.

CASTING

The role of War may be doubled with another male character, such as Costard or Berowne, to round out the cast to five men and five women. The cross-gender casting of the role of War, however, is not recommended.

SETS

A unit set with no movable parts and a large number of exits and entrances is strongly recommended to keep the action moving. A staircase can be extremely useful, especially for the dungeon scenes, but is not a requirement.

MUSIC

For pre-show and intermission music, I recommend Romantic music from the 19th century, mostly piano. For Jaquenetta's three songs, please listen to the early recordings of Bessie Smith and Billie Holiday for inspiration.

PROPS

The use of a period wheelchair is strongly recommended for the death of Longaville in Scene 12. But, if carefully choreographed, that moment can also take place with Longaville seated on a bench, next to Maria.

ACT ONE

PROLOGUE

(We hear the sounds of battle—a terrifying cacophony of boots stomping, rifles cracking, machine guns hammering, artillery bursting, biplanes roaring...)

(Enter WAR.)

WAR
Nay, do not run—for thou dost know me well;
Though now my clothes are torn, and my grim visage
Arrayed in blood. 'Twas only four years since
That thou didst take my hand and welcome me.
Why, is not this the very place that thou
Didst fold me in thy open arms, and kiss
My rosy cheeks, and praise my bearing much,
Swearing oaths and waving flags as I marched by?
And dost thou now not know me? O for shame!
Why, thou didst polish bright my silver buttons,
And sharpen my worn sword, and fill my purse
With borrowed gold and new-collected treasure.
And dost thou now not recognize my face?
I am war, the pandemonious child
You once adored, born in the self-same hour,
And in that same contagious bed whereon
The last French King commanded his last breath,
Whose sickness, carried on the wanton breeze,
Infected intertwined alliances
As fragile as a widow spider's web,
Infesting all the fecund courts of Europe
With deadly enmity. For four long years

I've toiled for thy glory without rest,
Deafening sons with my thunderous voice,
Defiling daughters with my fiery fists,
Trampling villages with my cruel boots,
Starving children with my greedy stomach,
Bereaving fathers with my stony heart,
Widowing wives with my venomous breath,
Divorcing bodies from their timeless souls,
And all in loving and devoted service
To thy most deep and secretive desires;
And dost thou now disown me? Call me bastard?
Spit out my bitter name? Well, 'tis no matter:
I know thou shalt despair when I am gone,
Which soon may come to pass, for now, alas,
The fickle coronets of Spain and France
Do court in Paris, where they woo and dance,
United by desire to conceive
A fetal treaty that will banish me
From out the skirts of these deflower'd lands.
But what care I if they expel me hence?
For I'm in great demand on every plot
Of this contentious ball of wormy earth.
Pretend then, henceforth, not to know my birth.
A round or two my labors here shall cease,
While Time gestates my witless sibling, peace.

(Exit WAR.)

SCENE I: THE ROYAL PALACE, PARIS

(In the distance, we hear a bell strike a melody of sixteen notes, then, after a brief pause, the hour of ONE.)

(As the clock chimes, ISABELLE, in tears, enters, followed by KATHERINE.)

KATHERINE
How now, dear princess Isabelle? Will war
Of old age perish and be laid to rest?
What says King Louis, your most royal brother,
To Spain's most recent offering of peace?

ISABELLE
Indeed, dear Katherine, another scheme
For armistice doth lie upon the table
Between the royalties of France and Spain,
Which may, by all reports, have better prospect
Of mutual acceptance than before.

KATHERINE
Why then, let us rejoice this welcome news!

ISABELLE
Most certainly these tidings cheer my heart.

KATHERINE
Why dost thou, then, seem so disconsolate?

ISABELLE
For that there is an article set down
In this agreement that doth grieve my heart
To contemplate.

KATHERINE
              What article is that?

ISABELLE
My royal brother and the King of Spain
Do now propose to settle their dispute

Over the kingdom of Navarre by splitting
Those lands in half by north and south,
Consuming it entirely between them.

KATHERINE
So then Navarre will vanish from the map?

ISABELLE
It seems there is no other way: for both
Do claim historic rights, and neither side
Will yield the bounty of those fruitful lands
To the possession of the enemy.

KATHERINE
A neccesary-painful bargain, then.
For if they should prolong this senseless war,
These kings would shed in vain the valiant blood
Of many valiant sons whose lives are spared
Through this imposed division of Navarre.

ISABELLE
Yea, cousin Kate, but with Navarre divided,
My fervent hopes to be once more united
With Ferdinand, Navarre's most worthy King,
Of dire wounds shall quickly fade and die,
For when he hears the news of this decree,
He never more will joy to look on me.

KATHERINE
Alas, King Ferdinand must needs be griev'd
By the sharp loss of country, crown, and kingdom;
And yet, the sea of letters from his grace
Proclaim his deep desire to see thy face.

ISABELLE
Alas, sweet coz, four years have interven'd

Since last I saw the King, and time, I fear,
Hath blunted the keen edge of his affections;
For his missives, whose every word did flow
Like liquid fire to fuse our fractured fortunes,
Now run as cool as doth a mountain stream
From off a snowy summit.

KATHERINE
                    Certainly
Four years of ceaseless war hath changed us all;
Yet even so, I do believe the vows
We did exchange in that same solemn hour
In which the news of your dear father's death
Did reach our ears, shall prosper and endure:
Not just between King Ferdinand and you,
But 'twixt the Lord Berowne and Rosaline,
Between Maria and Lord Longaville,
And 'twixt myself and loving Lord Dumaine.

ISABELLE
Your words of kindness overwhelm me, Kate.
But pardon me, my self-affected discourse!
What tidings from the dauntless Lord Dumaine?

KATHERINE
He sends me word that he will soon be here
To serve as Ferdinand's ambassador
At this our continental conference.

ISABELLE
'Tis said this surly war hath so befriended
The Lord Dumaine for bringing forth new weapons
To fortify the fatal aims of soldiers,
That untold wealth doth overflow his coffers.

KATHERINE
In sooth, the course of this accursèd war,
Hath been to him an unremitting blessing.

ISABELLE
And doth his lordship doggedly maintain
His amorous designs upon you, Kate?

KATHERINE
Yea, so much so, my lady, that he writes—
Emboldened, doubtless, by unchecked success—
As though I were a city under siege!
For lo, in missives most provocative,
He chargeth me, in terse offensive terms,
Prepare me for a pitiless assault
Upon my singular, unmanned estate.

ISABELLE
What? Doth the Monarch of Munitions make demands?
Then hast thou made a most inflammatory match!

KATHERINE
Indeed, I fear that, given his resolve
To take up arms against my maidenhood,
I no defense shall have but to surrender
To his firm will ere any shot be fired.

ISABELLE
Then we had best make ample preparation
For the campaign of the profane Dumaine!

KATHERINE
But hast thou heard a word from Rosaline?

ISABELLE
I've written letters to her many times,

Imploring her to make return to Paris,
But all of my entreaties failed to find her,
Returning home unopened and unread.

KATHERINE
How rash of her to run off to the war
And never send us word of her well-being!

ISABELLE
'Tis rumored she doth travel in disguise,
Impersonating manhood as a soldier
Embedded in the ranks of infantry.

KATHERINE
Our headstrong Rosaline, grunting and sweating
Under the weight of a drab uniform?
Never! Was it Maria told you so?

ISABELLE
I will not say Maria said as much,
For I have sworn to keep her confidence.

KATHERINE
Then well it may prove true, for our Maria
Is known for knowing more than she will say,
And saying greatly less than she doth know.

ISABELLE
And this repute hath garnered her a post
As diplomatic minister and counsel
To Louis at the treaty conference.

KATHERINE
Where she could speak at length, if she did choose,
Of every minute's closely-guarded news!

ISABELLE
How proud I am of her deserved success!

KATHERINE
And so am I, most proud, though I confess,
I wish that her discretion served her less!

ISABELLE
Look, here she comes!

KATHERINE *(Aside)*
                I pray she brings good tidings!

(Enter MARIA.)

MARIA
My gracious Princess, as you did request,
I've come to tell you that King Ferdinand
Hath just arrived in Paris with his train
And shortly shall be present in the court.

ISABELLE
O how I long for that same noble presence!

KATHERINE
Is Lord Dumaine with him?

MARIA
                'Tis said he is;
Moreover, I have heard that Lord Berowne,
A captain now in Ferdinand's battalions,
Is somewhere to be found within the palace.

ISABELLE
Captain Berowne? Is he here, too?

KATHERINE
                            What brings
The madcap Captain to our captivated court?

MARIA
I'm told he hath been wholly instrumental,
Since the rude trumpet of war first sounded,
In entertaining gravely-wounded soldiers
In tented hospitals along the raging front.

ISABELLE
How well he hath attended to his oath!
But knows he not his wayward Rosaline
Hath long been absent from the royal palace?

MARIA
I know not, Madam, though it has been said
He comes at the behest of Ferdinand,
Who seeks to reunite his trusted friends
To end this senseless war, and liberate
The all-too-long imprison'd Longaville.

ISABELLE
Alas, poor Longaville! For three long years,
My dear Maria, thou hast called upon him
In the dank dungeon of this palace, showing
Devotion well beyond the bounds of duty.
Is he in able health? How are his spirits?

MARIA
'Tis not a trial, but a joy, my Princess,
To visit with him in his cell each day,
To bring him learnèd books and earnest cheer,
And talk with him about man's suffering,
And learn from him the power of compassion;
And though his corporal health declines apace,

His spirits are robust; he seems content
To contemplate the workings of this world,
Within the confines of his little cell.

ISABELLE
Beshrew my brother's royal stubbornness
In holding him a prisoner so long!

MARIA
Not so, dear Isabelle! The King, in this,
Shows mercy: for though it was suspected
Lord Longaville did enter France in stealth
To infiltrate her borders as a spy,
For which the punishment is certain death,
The King doth keep him nourish'd and alive.

KATHERINE
He was a spy indeed, gentle Maria,
For keeping still his oath a twelvemonth old
To come before his love and challenge her,
He risked his death in crossing enemy lines
To spy his dearest love, and infiltrate
The limits of her barricaded heart.

MARIA
For which my love for him is limitless.

KATHERINE
Then let us pray that these three noble Kings
Of lasting peace will make a strong accord,
And with their civil pens vanquish the sword!

ISABELLE
Shall we seek out these men and give them greeting?

KATHERINE
Let's go to them at once, for time is fleeting!

MARIA
And may good fortune bless our happy meeting!

(Exit ISABELLE, KATHERINE, and MARIA.)

SCENE 2: THE GREAT HALL

(Enter COSTARD.)

COSTARD
Through the palace have I gone, but Berowne found I not.

FERDINAND *(Heard in the distance, offstage)*
Costard!

COSTARD
Though, this is not surprising. For the eye that I have left, the right, sees not the right way to go. You'd think my right eye would seek the right way, but my right eye doth miss the left so terribly, was so in love with the left, that since the left left, the right doth little but ache for the left, and naught goes right.

DUMAINE *(Heard in the distance, offstage)*
Costard!

COSTARD
As for my legs, the good leg I have left, the right, strives to do the right thing. But the bad leg, the left, or what's left of it, hath no goodness left in him, can't stand to do the right thing. Whenever I favor the good leg to get ahead, the bad leg grows peevish, drags its heels—or heel—tries to knock me off my feet,

so that my gait never lets me get to the tavern, or the path, or even past the gate.

FERDINAND *(Getting closer, from offstage)*
Costard!

COSTARD
In truth, there's no one to blame but I, myself. For if I'd merely stepped to the right instead of to the left, I'd be standing here now with two good eyes, two good legs, and two good *(holds his crotch)*—

DUMAINE *(Much closer now, from offstage)*
Costard!

COSTARD:
Well, I thank the Lord above I still have both my ears!

(Exit COSTARD in one direction, as FERDINAND and DUMAINE enter from another.)

FERDINAND
Nay, do not speak of patience, good Dumaine!
Shall I sit idly by while France and Spain
Devour the hapless kingdom of Navarre
As doth two lion cubs a fallen deer,
Tearing the tender meat from off her bones
And leaving nothing but a rotten carcass
To be inhabited by worms and maggots?

DUMAINE
My sovereign lord—

FERDINAND
Nay, thou dost mock me, Lord Dumaine;

I am no sovereign! I have no crown,
No nation, no people, no land, no—Costard!

COSTARD *(Re-entering from a different direction)*
Here, my noble lord.

FERDINAND
Costard, thou shirksome rogue! Where hast thou been?

COSTARD
Dogging mine own shadow in this labyrinth of a palace!

DUMAINE
What? Didst thou navigate the fires of hell
To lose thy way in corridors of marble?

COSTARD
Forgive me, gracious lord, for though my body hath left the battlefield, the battlefield hath not left my body.

FERDINAND
But hast thou yet encountered Lord Berowne?
He sent us word that he would meet us here.

COSTARD
I found brave Hercules, my liege, but saw not Lord Berowne.

DUMAINE
What? Didst thou encounter Hercules?

COSTARD
Yea, my good lord, as hard as marble, standing guard in the garden; missing a limb, but what he lacked in limberness, he made up for with his swollen club, which he held over his head to impress upon his mistress, Venus.

DUMAINE
What, didst thou come upon the goddess Venus?

COSTARD
Indeed, I did; I discovered her half naked on the half shell, beckoning Hercules to help her find her lost virginity.

DUMAINE
In one of the garden beds?

COSTARD
Just so, my lord, just so—buried down a hole.

DUMAINE
A mole's hole?

COSTARD
Nay, nay—'twas a hare's lair.

DUMAINE
A weasel's den.

COSTARD
A badger's nest.

DUMAINE
A fox's burrow.

COSTARD
A snake's pit.

DUMAINE
A skunk's spelunk!

FERDINAND
Nay, cease this beastly banter, I beseech thee!

Costard, resume your search for Lord Berowne,
And send him to us when you do unearth him.

COSTARD
I shall ferret him out, my liege, wherever he may be!

(Exit COSTARD.)

FERDINAND
For shame, Dumaine! I would you would refrain
From spurring on the muddy-minded Costard
To needless and circuitous distractions.
Our calling here is of too stern a nature
To wile away the time in bawdy discourse.

DUMAINE
Forgive me, liege, for I'm a man of business,
And I have found that business savors best
When seasoned with a modicum of pleasure.

FERDINAND
I take no pleasure in the tasks we face,
Saving Navarre from bifurcated theft
And ransoming enfetter'd Longaville,
For 'tis employment void of any joy.

DUMAINE
Surely the King will joy in setting eyes,
After the passage of so many years,
Upon the lovely Isabelle of France?

FERDINAND
Indeed, I shall rejoice to see the Princess,
But doubt that she will joy to look on me.
And why should she?

DUMAINE
                    Alack, why should she not?
Her letters sent devotedly to you throughout
The war do tender her most tender thoughts.

FERDINAND
Why should the Princess care a whit for me,
Since I no longer am a royal king,
But come to her a beggar and a fool?

DUMAINE
A beggar and a fool, my gracious lord?

FERDINAND
A supplicant, who comes in on his knees
To beg her royal brother for his mercy,
To bauble and to jest for his largess.

DUMAINE
Methinks 'tis likely Princess Isabelle
Will take our part in brokering a peace.

FERDINAND
I grant thee that she stands our only hope.

DUMAINE
No, there is another—for Katherine,
The much belovèd cousin of King Louis,
Doth also wield some influence in court.

FERDINAND
Belov'd of Louis, and of Lord Dumaine,
Is it not so?

DUMAINE
                    'Tis so, my loving liege,

And for her love, I'd challenge all the world,
Though all the world defy my right possession.

FERDINAND
Thou dost possess a most possessive love,
My Lord Dumaine.

(Enter COSTARD.)

COSTARD
My liege, I found not Lord Berowne, but dug up more majestic
flesh and bones.

(Enter ISABELLE, KATHERINE, and MARIA.)

FERDINAND *(Aside)*
Sweet Isabelle!

DUMAINE *(Aside)*
      Enchanting Katherine!

(MARIA steps forward.)

MARIA
Most gracious Ferdinand and honor'd Lord Dumaine,
As diplomatic minister and counsel
To royal Louis, sovereign of France,
It is my pleasure and my privilege to express
His Highness' warmest welcome to the court,
And to extend his earnest invitation
To meet with him, with all convenient haste,
To formalize the terms of armistice.

DUMAINE
The hangman bids thee meet him up the stair
For that he has some pressing noose to share.

FERDINAND
My good Dumaine, I prithee now be silent.
The bluntness of your speech doth ill-become
An embassage of delicance and prudence.

DUMAINE
I beg your gentle pardon, good my liege,
Thou know'st it is my wont to render up
A naughty line to bring about mine ends.

COSTARD
Nay, 'tis the hangman renders up a knotty line to bring about his ends.

DUMAINE
Indeed! 'Twas a well-executed jest.

COSTARD
Then must thou pardon the offender.

DUMAINE
As soon as thou dost end thy sentence.

FERDINAND
I charge thee both to rein thy surly tongues!

COSTARD
Methinks 'tis time to drop the matter.

DUMAINE
Yea, 'tis a grave matter and therefore must expire.

COSTARD
Amen then, let it rest in peace.

FERDINAND
Peace, I say! Magnanimous Maria,
Thou dost conduct thine office admirably
To warble so in gentle dove-like tones
The disharmonious music of the crow;
And though my heart, to see you now, doth joy,
It grieves me, too, to be so gracefully enjoined
To join King Louis at the treaty table
To watch him carve Navarre as his dessert
And serve it as a dish for seated kings.

KATHERINE
Good King, though I speak out of turn to say it,
Be not so griev'd; Navarre must ne'er conclude
He hath no friends in France, for there are those
That 'gainst a world of kings do ready stand
To take the part of royal Ferdinand.

COSTARD *(Aside)*
From two of the triumvirate we've heard;
Shall we hear proclamations from the third?

FERDINAND
What, stand'st thou silent, royal Isabelle?
How shall the ramparts of my war-proof ears
Interpret the unspoken poetry
So eloquently sounded in thine eyes?

ISABELLE
Most royal Ferdinand, for four long years
I have rehearsed this very moment, practic'd
Before my glass what I would say, consider'd
Each gesture and inflection, repeated
Their diligent fulfillment in my sleep,
So I might give you a reception
Befitting this long-dreamt-upon reunion;

And yet, in this anticipated instant,
The woman that you see before you now
Is not a princess, but an artless child;
For catching sight of you doth so o'erwhelm
My sensibility and sense that all
Consideration, practice, repetition
Do melt away, and leave me wholly speechless.

FERDINAND
Speechless, dear Isabelle, you need not be;
For though the waging of this wasteful war
Hath left our coffers destitute and barren,
Yet have I ample store of speeches left
To lend my loving friends, as thus:
Item: speech for a princess to petition
A heartless king for genuine compassion;
Item: speech for a sister to implore
A stubborn brother for leniency;
Item: speech for a woman to entreat
A ravenous man for generosity.
I'll freely grant you any of these speeches
If thou wilt, in return, employ thy regal voice
To melt the heart of France on my behalf.

ISABELLE
Alas, upon the subject of the treaty,
My younger brother Louis, made impatient
By the incessant pressing of his sister,
Hath ruled I must not cry, nor plead, nor bend
My royal knee to champion your cause;
I therefore, for my silence, beg your patience,
For I on your behalf no tongue possess
To influence the King to give redress.

FERDINAND
Then are my labors lost, and my poor country
Condemn'd to be dissevered from the map.

MARIA
Not so, my royal lord; the armistice
Is not yet 'greed upon, and there is time
To press your strong objections to the pact
Among the league of nations here assembled.

FERDINAND
Might I peruse a copy of the treaty?

MARIA
I have one here for you to look upon.

(FERDINAND and MARIA step upstage to confer.)

DUMAINE
Most radiant and exquisite Katherine,
Beholding your ethereal appearance
Is like beholding, blazoned in the sky,
A second sunrise, brighter than the first.

KATHERINE
Two suns? Then surely doomsday is at hand!

DUMAINE
Not doomsday, Kate, and yet, a day of reckoning.
For surely thou shalt have two blessèd suns;
Two daughters, too, if thou wilt first have me.

KATHERINE
Have you? How? As an owl doth have a mouse?

DUMAINE
Ay, in the moonlight in the woods behind the barn.

KATHERINE
I' th' sunlight in the stocks behind the jail.

DUMAINE
Such punishment I would endure for thee.

KATHERINE
Such punishment thou dost inflict on me.

DUMAINE
Surrender, Kate, and I will show thee mercy.

KATHERINE
To hear thee sound retreat would be a mercy.

DUMAINE
Withdraw? Pull out? Unthinkable! And yet,
If you will meet the thrust of my demands,
I shall suspend hostilities for thee
And offer tender-hearted leniency.

KATHERINE
Will you lay down your arms, then, and relent?

DUMAINE
Ay, and my legs, dear Kate, if you consent.

(FERDINAND and MARIA step forward.)

FERDINAND
Then let us to the conference go at once
To win the hearts of other heads of state.

MARIA
Perchance your Highness is with travel tired;
May't please you first to view your royal chambers
To clear thy weary mind before this meeting?

DUMAINE
Shall we be lodg'd as is Lord Longaville:
Locked up and left to languish in a cell?

MARIA
Lord Longaville, you both may rest assur'd,
Though captive, is both comfortable and well;
For I have taken it upon myself,
These thousand days, to guard his health and safety,
Ensuring he be treated with respect
And dignity, as suits his noble stature.
Therefore, you need not fear, good Lord Dumaine,
For thou shalt find thy lodgings most humane.

FERDINAND
We thank you heartily for your good care
Of our most dear and long-enfetter'd friend.

DUMAINE
When may we visit him?

MARIA
                         None but the King
May grant a visitation to his cell.

DUMAINE
Then let us to King Louis' side with speed
To snatch the keys and see our brother freed.

MARIA
I'll take you to his Highness presently.

FERDINAND
                              Costard,
Come not along with us, but seek out Lord Berowne.

COSTARD
Dost thou know, Maria, where I might find the man?

MARIA
Methinks he doth rehearse, with his associate,
This evening's entertainment in the ballroom.

FERDINAND
Find out the ballroom, then, and bring us Lord Berowne.

COSTARD
I'll bring him thence though he were posted on the moon!

(Exit FERDINAND, DUMAINE, ISABELLE, MARIA, and KATHERINE. Exit COSTARD separately.)

SCENE 3: A BALLROOM IN THE PALACE

(Enter ROSALINE, reading a letter.)

ROSALINE
"My dearest Rosaline, I crave thy counsel
And sage advice on grave affairs of state;
Return, therefore, with all convenient speed,
To Paris, where the crownèd heads of Europe
Do congregate to arbitrate a treaty."
Obeying thus the will of my dear Princess,
I dutifully have returned to Paris;
But yet I do remain in this disguise,
A correspondent armed with ink and pen,

Wherein I boldly counterfeit a man,
For in it, I have seen with mine own eyes
The field of battle; heard with mine own ears
The sound of skirmish, smelled with mine own nose
The stench of death, and with these faculties,
Made sharp upon the whetstone of this war,
I hope to witness these hostilities
Protracted in a gentlemanly fashion,
Exchanging smoke-filled rooms for smoke-filled skies,
Dull statesmanship for lethal marksmanship,
Long tables for deep trenches, tired phrases
For tired forces, folded arms for loaded arms,
And write all down to share with all the world.
I'll stay, therefore, a man, until that time
When war's death knells, and bells of peace do chime.
But who is he comes here? It is Berowne!

(ROSALINE steps aside. Enter BEROWNE and JAQUENETTA.)

BEROWNE
This ballroom, Jaquenetta, shall be the venue for your act. 'Tis a stage fit for a command performance!

JAQUENETTA
I shall scarce know how to sing, with walls to keep out wind, and a roof to keep out rain.

BEROWNE
Thou need'st not fear, dear Jaq, for the lords o' th' court shall provide the wind, and the ladies the rain.

JAQUENETTA
How's that, Berowne?

BEROWNE
The men shall speak rudely while you attempt to sing, filling

the room with biting gusts, and the women will cry when they hear your mournful tunes, filling the room with salt tears.

JAQUENETTA
Alack, with so much wind and water, love, 'twill be a torrent. I shall sing them, therefore, only songs of joy tonight; 'twill keep us warm and dry.

BEROWNE
Nay, do not so; rather sing them only songs of war and loss, of chaos and destruction, of woeful events and disastrous happenings, that they shall fear to drown in a deluge of despair.

JAQUENETTA
Wherefore should I stir up such deadly weather?

BEROWNE
So shall you move them, like Noah, to embark upon an ark of armistice lest they should perish in a new great flood.

JAQUENETTA
Yea, two of every sort: the foul and the beastly.

BEROWNE
Ay, male and female, side by side. Then let us hear a woeful ballad fit for our tempestuous designs.

(BEROWNE places a microphone stand on the stage.)

JAQUENETTA
'Twill make you melancholy, lover.

BEROWNE
Truly, it shall. But 'tis no matter; sing.

(As JAQUENETTA sings, BEROWNE is observed closely—sometimes too closely!—by ROSALINE.)

JAQUENETTA *(Singing)*
I still recall our last goodbye
As if 'twere only yesterday;
For it was when we said goodbye
I began to feel this way.

(BEROWNE takes out his flask and begins drinking...)

I've said adieu so many times
To friends and lovers I once knew,
There's only one I can't forget—
Bidding farewell to you.

(BEROWNE looks at the sky, lost in a reverie...)

The sky was clear, the stars did shine,
The night was perfect for romance,
So when we heard the music play
Our hearts surrendered to the dance.

(BEROWNE offers his hand to an imagined Rosaline and begins to dance with her...)

We laughed and kissed as we did sway,
I thought the night would never end,
So when the music stopped, my dear,
My poor heart failed to comprehend.

(BEROWNE stops dancing; he wanders restlessly, drinking...)

Our last goodbye, our last goodbye,
Our last goodbye, our last goodbye.

(BEROWNE takes a photo of Rosaline from his pocket; he gazes at it, kisses it...)

So when I see you once again,
If that should ever be my fate,
I'll bid the music play once more,
And this time I won't hesitate.

(BEROWNE tucks the photo back into his pocket; he sits and continues drinking...)

I'll take your hand, and hold you tight,
We'll dance until the morning light,
And I'll make sure our last goodbye
Will be our last goodbye,
Will be our last goodbye,
Our last goodbye.

BEROWNE
Ah, 'tis a beautiful song; I prithee, Jaq, who wrote it?

JAQUENETTA
You did, lover.

BEROWNE
Did I so? Then drink I to the wretched author!

JAQUENETTA
Such toasts will bloat the author's head most wretchedly.

BEROWNE
'Tis true, but who will notice in these times of wretchedness?

JAQUENETTA
Ah, marry, that will I.

BEROWNE
Then must you quaff as well.

JAQUENETTA
Nay, we know what happens when I quaff as well, don't we, lover?

BEROWNE:
That's Captain Lover to you, if thou speak'st against my drink.

JAQUENETTA:
Ay, ay, then Captain; I'll abandon you before your ship dost sink.

(Exit JAQUENETTA.)

BEROWNE
For shame, Berowne! Must thou in sport abuse
Poor Jaquenetta thus? 'Tis not her fault
Thou canst not love her. Since the war began,
She hath been loyal, patient, understanding,
Offering her kindness and her constancy
From one end of the compass to the other;
Without resentment, shivering in the cold,
Without complaining, plodding though the mud,
Without a grumble, wanting for a meal,
Without objection, roasting in the sun,
Without an outcry, slumb'ring on the ground,
And yet—poor doting fool!—I cannot love her,
For only thoughts of loving Rosaline
Enthrall my mind and push out all thoughts else.
If only I could disabuse my heart
Of her I am without for her I'm with!

(ROSALINE steps forward to reveal herself.)

ROSALINE
I prithee, soldier, dost thou know Berowne,
The captain that brings forth a show tonight?

BEROWNE
I know Berowne; who is it that doth seek him?

ROSALINE
In print, I'm called Emmanuel Lanier.

BEROWNE
I know thee not in print, but in the flesh
Thou look'st familiar. I am Berowne.
Did not I speak with thee in Bordeaux once?

ROSALINE
Did not I speak with thee in Bordeaux once?

BEROWNE
'Tis likely, for I often seek out solace
In Bordeaux, in Cognac, and in Champagne.

ROSALINE
I see thou lead'st a spirited existence.

BEROWNE
Indeed, my life is most intoxicating.

ROSALINE
I heard thee give an entertaining speech
To wounded troops beneath a tent in Bordeaux;
Thou made'st them roar until their sides did split.

BEROWNE
How rude it was of me to wound them further.

ROSALINE
'Twas rumored 'mongst the soldiers you did vow
To ease the sick and dying with your wit
To win a woman who did spurn your love.

BEROWNE
This rumor is a double-dealing wench, who vows
To hold her tongue while naked on her back,
But up and dressed doth her affairs unpack.

ROSALINE
Wilt thou bestow a witty speech tonight?

BEROWNE
My comic acts shall no more see the light.

ROSALINE
And why is that?

BEROWNE
                For that I've surely found
That laughter cannot save men from the ground.

(Enter COSTARD.)

COSTARD
Good e'en, good sirs: doth either of you know where I might find—Captain Berowne! Very well met! I was sent to seek you out!

BEROWNE
And thou hast found me, my most forward scout.
Let me inspect thee! How art thou, Corporal?

COSTARD
My corporal soundness hath experienced some corporal

sufferance affecting my corporal motion, but otherwise, my corporal appetites have not abated and my spirits are fine!

BEROWNE
Enough of this corporal punishment, I beseech thee! Where are the King and Lord Dumaine?

COSTARD
They are here in court, sir, and do require your company haste-post-haste.

BEROWNE
Then let us post at once; for there's no post to waste!

COSTARD
I'll lead the way!

(Exit BEROWNE and COSTARD.)

ROSALINE
Alack, my lord is in a forlorn state;
The task I set for him hath been too harsh,
For it hath robbed him of his natural mirth.
How arrogant and cruel it was of me
To send him on a quest of self-destruction,
Seeking to slay the triple-headed dragon
Of anguish, misery, and desperation
To prove that he is worthy of my love.
Alas, what shall I do to make amends?
I must embrace a way to right this wrong;
Four years of doing penance is too long!
I shall seek out the Princess.

(Exit ROSALINE.)

SCENE 4: THE PALACE DUNGEON

(In the darkness, we hear a heavy steel door being slammed shut and locked tight.)

(Enter LONGAVILLE and MARIA.)

LONGAVILLE
Sweet Maria, I thank thee for these books;
Your loving-kindness nothing overlooks,
For every printed line of these worn pages
Contains the ancient wisdom of the sages,
Whose simple eloquence doth carry me
Upon a breeze of sweet philosophy
That lifts me o'er these walls beyond all sight
To break the bonds of earth in joyous flight.

MARIA
I would each sentence were a plumèd wing
So thou mightst fly the sentence of the king.

LONGAVILLE
The sentence of the king, though most perverse,
Hath been a blessing to me, not a curse,
For freedom's loss hath granted me a peace
That did infuse me once desire did cease,
And by embracing nothingness I find
That all of suffering is in the mind.

MARIA
Prepare your mind, then, gentle Longaville,
To bear the brunt of further sufferance still.

LONGAVILLE
Tell me thy news; I prithee, what hath passed?

MARIA
It grieves my heart to be the player cast
As messenger to bring you such ill-tidings.

LONGAVILLE
Say what you must; I shall attend with patience.

MARIA
I come with proclamations from King Louis,
Whom even now doth storm like moody Zeus
After Prometheus did steal immortal fire.

LONGAVILLE
And what hath angered him?

MARIA
                              King Ferdinand,
For daring to obstruct the armistice.

LONGAVILLE
Obstruct it how?

MARIA
                     He hath refused to sign,
Demanding your immediate release
Before he will debate his nation's fate.

LONGAVILLE
And what hath France, to answer this, proclaim'd?

MARIA
An answer that shall make our nation sham'd.
King Louis, after long deliberation,

Hath regally decreed thou art a spy,
And handeth down, by me, this bitter sentence:
Thou must prepare thy perishable body
Come break of day, for sudden execution.

LONGAVILLE
I fear not death, nor his ordain'd embrace,
For well death knows this cell I occupy;
For look you, every night I summon him
To cross my stony threshold, and to sit,
So I may gaze into his vacant face
While he doth gently tutor me, explaining
That what we mortals think of as our end
Is not an end at all, no, not a whit,
For he doth show me how I shall abide
In plants, in beasts, in sea, in field, in sky,
Whereby I've found the master key to peace
Is to allow ourselves to treasure death,
To welcome him into our ring of friends,
And be at ease with his determined ends.

MARIA
Thou leap'st to this conclusion far too fast!
This sunset shall not be thy very last,
For France, to show his mercy most divine,
Is willing to revoke thy lethal fine.

LONGAVILLE
What must I do to shake his fatal blame?

MARIA
Convince King Ferdinand to sign his name.

LONGAVILLE
I cannot ask my King to counterpoise
The execution of his friend against

The imminent extinction of Navarre;
Not for the world.

MARIA
                And why is that, my love?

LONGAVILLE
'Tis not for me to influence events;
The best way is to let things run their course.

MARIA
The course, my lord, already hath been run:
The war shall end; Navarre shall be undone;
And Ferdinand shall lose his royal crown;
There is no need to see his friend cut down.
Convince Navarre of this, and win release;
Thus ends this war, and thus begins a peace.

LONGAVILLE
'Tis but the blindness of mankind to see
The steady swirling of the universe
In endings and beginnings. But the river
Of history hath not a source,
And never shall it reach the sea;
It twists and turns and will not be controll'd
By clumps of earth like me. I therefore choose
To step aside and let its fluid course
Fashion a channel as befits its nature.

MARIA
Doth thou not see? Thou shalt be swept away
And drowned by history. And to what end?
Navarre shall be consumed by France and Spain,
And I'll be left behind to mourn you slain.

LONGAVILLE
The nature of my death means not a jot;
Our time will pass, and all will be forgot.

MARIA
Our time? What time? We've had no time to spend
Beyond these heartless walls. For when did we
Have time for lusty walks? And when did we
Have time to raise a child? And when did we
Have time to laugh, to feast, to dance, to sail,
Enjoying life together till we're frail?

LONGAVILLE
'Tis true; we've not had time to do these things;
And yet we have enjoyed a thousand days
Of kindness, generosity, and love
Within this strong enclosure, for the which
We must give thanks, rather than curse the loss
Of what was never promis'd, never owed.

MARIA
You will not help me free you from this plight?

LONGAVILLE
I shall remain unmov'd throughout this night.

MARIA
I cannot watch you die, and must persist.

LONGAVILLE
And I accept what is, and won't resist.

MARIA
Once more I'll urge the King thy life to spare.

LONGAVILLE
Once more, dear heart, I'll urge thee to forbear;
For nothing whatsoever is amiss,
And I desire no more life than this.

MARIA
Then with this kiss, I'll leave the rest unsaid.

LONGAVILLE
And now, I needs must rest my weary head.

MARIA
Then sleep, my dear one, sleep.

(LONGAVILLE sleeps.)

Alas, I have depleted him with pleading,
And must conceive a new way of proceeding.
These kings face off as in a game of chess,
Both players full of pride and stubbornness,
And Longaville is but a lowly pawn
That shall be sacrificed by break of dawn.
I must devise a gambit of such awe
That shall compel the game unto a draw.
But how? How shall I hold them both in check
To keep the noose from off my lover's neck?
Whate'er it be, the next move on the board is mine,
And for my mate's sake, I will not resign.

(Exit MARIA.)

SCENE 5: THE PALACE GARDENS

(Enter DUMAINE with KATHERINE.)

KATHERINE
Why must we speak so urgently i' th' garden,
When all is chaos and commotion in the court?
Louis doth fume; the Princess is distraught;
Maria doth despair, and Ferdinand
Doth storm about the palace like Poseidon
Seeking to drown all France beneath a raging sea.
I must return apace before I'm miss'd.

DUMAINE
Thou hast been sorely miss'd, dear Katherine, by me,
Which instantly I mean to remedy.

KATHERINE
'Tis shameful, lord, to pull me thus away,
And box me in this bold and sudden manner.

DUMAINE
Tis neither bold nor sudden, gracious Kate.
Four years ago, thou chargest me to come
And challenge thee, which even now I do,
For I have served thee faithfully and true.

KATHERINE
To speak of love, Dumaine, and wedded bliss,
The time and place are very much amiss.

DUMAINE
Nay, time and place will serve our turn indeed,
For I have hired them and paid their wages,

And now they both do wear my livery,
And shall discharge at once their master's will.

KATHERINE
Then bid your servants both, for goodness' sake,
Attend their master's will later and elsewhere.

DUMAINE
Later and elsewhere do not work for me;
But now, dear Katherine, here, on bended knee,
I ask: wilt thou consent to wear this ring?

KATHERINE
It cannot be, for if this timid finger
Doth give consent to such a precious gift,
My other digits would prove jealous rivals,
Desiring to be treasur'd in like fashion;
One hand shall fight the other for thy love,
One ear the other ear; yea, my bare neck
Shall squabble with my unadornèd breast,
Hoping for a token of thy esteem;
Therefore, to keep the peace, I must say no
To stay the feud that 'tween my parts would grow.

DUMAINE
Nay, every part of thy exquisite frame
Shall bear a token of my dear devotion;
From every graceful limb and supple branch
Of thy majestic tree shall hang, like precious buds,
The cultivated issue of my love,
Where they shall bloom and grow, like ripen'd fruit,
Soaking up the sunlight of my affection.

KATHERINE
Enough! No more! Here stands thy fallen tree,

And thou my nurturing arborist shall be.
Here is my hand.

(He places the ring on her finger. They almost kiss. Enter ISABELLE.)

ISABELLE
How now, dear Katherine! Where hast thou been?
I do require your presence in my chambers.

KATHERINE
Forgive me, gracious Princess; I attend.
(Aside to DUMAINE)
I must be gone; I prithee save that kiss
Till we do celebrate the armistice.

(Exit KATHERINE and ISABELLE.)

DUMAINE
Nay, do not judge; for there's no person here
That hath not purchas'd love with something dear;
True partnerships are framed by Him above,
But jewels are the currency of love;
Thus do I consummate a goodly sport
That shall beget a place in France's court.
The end of war is near; it must be so,
The end of profit is not certain though;
For if I lose my factories in Navarre,
My wealth is safely stored in vaults afar;
And if my nation-state doth not endure,
My marriage vows to Katherine keep me sure.
Let him who would do otherwise be cross;
For life's too short to suffer such a loss.

(Enter FERDINAND.)

FERDINAND
An arrogant, ill-temper'd, pock-faced boy!
The king of cockroaches, monarch of butterflies,
Sovereign of salamanders, snails, and sponges!
A lisping, capering, castrato of a king
Unfit to sit upon a chamber pot,
Much less a royal throne. A toddler tyrant!
And dare he threaten? Dare he make demands?
They'll find his Lowness drown'd in his cold oatmeal
Before I shall relent to such extortion.

DUMAINE
My liege, this tirade doth not profit us,
Nor saves Navarre, nor spares Lord Longaville.
The time is running short, and options thin;
We must pursue our recourse with some discipline.
What says the Princess to your last appeal?

FERDINAND
To my entreaties she is hard as steel.

DUMAINE
And have we access to the cell of Longaville?

FERDINAND
Maria cannot sway King Louis' will.

DUMAINE
What then of our undaunted Lord Berowne?

FERDINAND
We hope to hear his golden counsel soon.

(Enter COSTARD and BEROWNE.)

COSTARD
Ah, here they are, my Captain!

BEROWNE
At last, you damnable, misleading slave!
Odysseus took a more direct route home
To Ithaca, than thou to bring me hither!

COSTARD
If thou art Odysseus, then must I be the Cyclops.

FERDINAND
My Lord Berowne, I joy to see thy face.
Come, let me clutch thee!

COSTARD
And here is thy Penelope!

BEROWNE
My royal liege, I've missed thy royal presence.

COSTARD
(*Aside*) Thy cellars full of wine, thy roasted pheasants.

BEROWNE
Dumaine! Thou dost look stouter now than in the past.

DUMAINE
And thou look'st older, Cap, than when I saw you last.

BEROWNE
Yea, I have aged, Dumaine, like Gorgonzola cheese.

COSTARD
(*Aside*) Chas'd down with a barrel of Bourbon, if you please.

FERDINAND
Four years of war, my friends, hath aged us all.

DUMAINE
But Longaville the most, no doubt; poor man,
He hath not seen the sky in three full years.

BEROWNE
Costard hath told me of his mortal plight.
Shall he be executed at first light?

FERDINAND
Yea, that the despot Louis hath decreed.

BEROWNE
A way to save his life is what we need;
Did'st thou not offer ransom for his freedom?

DUMAINE
I offer'd payment worthy of a king,
But Louis hath refus'd each proffered sum.

FERDINAND
To our entreaties he will not succumb;
He only will accept my signature
According France a portion of Navarre.

DUMAINE
That cannot be! For if we lose Navarre
We'll live out all our lives in infamy.

FERDINAND
What say you then, Berowne? Give us some counsel
To save our names from living on in shame.

BEROWNE
Then here it is: if gold will not suffice
To save our friend, I'll offer up my life
To Louis in exchange for Longaville's.
For greater love than this no man expends:
To lay down his own life to save his friend's.

FERDINAND
And so shall I then.

DUMAINE
                              Yea, so shall we all!
(Aside) This foolish action I must needs forestall!

BEROWNE
Then onward, fearless soldiers, to King Louis!

FERDINAND
We'll save our loyal friend, come what come may,
And may the people of Navarre observe this day!
Costard, lead the way!

(Exit ALL.)

SCENE 6: THE GREAT HALL

(Enter ISABELLE, KATHERINE, MARIA, and ROSALINE, still disguised.)

ROSALINE
They should be harshly punish'd, not rewarded,
For launching such an all-destructive war,
Imposing so much misery and loss
Upon the batter'd populace of Europe.

MARIA
I understand your views, Monsieur Lanier,
But surely, sir, these punitive conditions,
These savage reparations and partitions,
Will do far more to aggravate the wounds
Inflicted by this war than they shall heal;
For an infectious discontent shall spread
And grow to be the source of further bloodshed;
No, clemency and pardon's best for all;
Vindictiveness shall start another brawl.

KATHERINE
For my part, I believe that war, like love,
Plays not by any rules, and consequently,
There is no profit to be made in talking,
After the game is over, about fairness;
For, by this hand, I swear—

ISABELLE
                    Nay, hold!
What dost thou wear, pray tell, upon thy finger?

KATHERINE
The Lord Dumaine presented me this ring
As an expression of his boundless love.

MARIA
'Tis an engagement ring?

ISABELLE
                    From Lord Dumaine?

MARIA
An emerald confin'd by diamonds!

ROSALINE
Yea, purchas'd with the lives of innocents.

KATHERINE
Nay, given to me by a noble prince.

ROSALINE
These jewels are the fruits of violence—
A ring of precious stones soaked in the blood
Of precious mothers, fathers, daughters, sons,
The windfall from the fall of villages,
The surplus earned of burning homes and farms,
The yield of soldier-spattered battlefields,
The profits of privation, pain, and death.
How canst thou wear so sinister a thing
Upon thy finger as this tainted ring?

KATHERINE
Alas, what can I do by way of remedy?
The pow'r to right these wrongs rests not with me.

ROSALINE
Thou hast a greater power than thou know'st,
For thou canst hit him where it hurts him most.

KATHERINE
And where is that?

ROSALINE
            Upon his manly vanity
And pride; therefore, you must return the ring
With this demand: if he would marry you,
He must agree to halt the sale of armaments.

ISABELLE
Nay more, he must agree to disassemble
All those munitions presently in store.

MARIA
Still more: he must agree to give away
His ill-gained profits to the wretched poor.

KATHERINE
And if he will not? What shall I do then?

MARIA
As Lysistrata did for warring Athens,
So thou shalt do for continental Europe.

ISABELLE
Thou shalt withhold thy feminine affections
Till he disarms his menacing erections.

MARIA
Dost thou agree to this our peaceful scheme?

KATHERINE
Indeed, I do concur; it seems I must,
For Lord Dumaine's designs I cannot trust.

(Enter COSTARD.)

COSTARD
Good e'en, good gentlewomen. I prithee, can you tell me,
which is the way to the royal throne room?

ROSALINE
Thou'rt not the first, nor will not be the last,
To lose his way in seeking out the throne!

COSTARD
Mistress Rosaline? How glad I am to find you! I have a letter for you that I have longèd long to see delivered.

(COSTARD searches his pockets.)

ROSALINE
I fear you are mistaken, gentle friend;
I am not whom you seem to think I am.

COSTARD
Mistaken? Nay, I am not mistaken! I have taken you for Rosaline, and so you are. With organ pipes like thine, I'd take you anywhere. Under enemy fire, I'd take you. Beneath a blasting canon, I'd take you. Behind a marching band, I'd take you. 'Tis certain you are Rosaline.

ISABELLE
How now?

KATHERINE
    Our Rosaline?

MARIA
        Can it be so?

KATHERINE
Disguisèd as a man?

(KATHERINE removes ROSALINE's hat.)

ISABELLE
    'Tis Rosaline indeed!

ROSALINE
This purblind fool hath seen right through my dress!
Guilty, guilty as charg'd, I do confess;
My manly manner now I do resign;
I am, in sooth, your wayward Rosaline
Come home to Paris, as you did entreat,
Whom here, in trousers, kneeling at thy feet,
Appealing to the judge's leniency,
Doth beg forgiveness for deceiving thee.

ISABELLE
Then tell the jury, leaving nothing out,
Upon thine honor, how this came about.

MARIA
Spare no detail!

KATHERINE
     We needs must hear it all!

ROSALINE
I'll tell you first to last what did befall.
I conjured up Emmanuel Lanier—

COSTARD
Here 'tis! here 'tis! I knew that it was here!

(COSTARD gives ROSALINE a yellowing, crumpled paper.)

ROSALINE
How long hast thou been carrying this post?

COSTARD
Let's see: two years perhaps, or three at most.

KATHERINE
From Lord Berowne?

ROSALINE
        Ay, even so.

ISABELLE
              What is't?

ROSALINE
A clipping from a newspaper—yea, three years old.

ISABELLE *(Reads)*
"Yet nowhere have I seen a finer example of grace and good humor under fire than beholding Captain Berowne's comedic performance continue without a flinch or pause during a fearful enemy barrage."

MARIA *(Reads)*
"The Captain's charitable works in military hospitals throughout Europe, cheering the speechless sick, amusing groaning wretches, and coaxing the painèd impotent to smile, surely qualify him for commendation as one of the great unsung heroes of this conflict."

KATHERINE
He hath fulfilled his promise to you admirably.

ROSALINE
But was there not a letter, Corporal Costard,
To penetrate the meaning of this missive?

COSTARD
Nay, there was none. But, if you have desire, it would pleasure him to penetrate his post for you himself; for he is hard by somewhere in the palace.

ROSALINE
Yea, I did bandy with him earlier today.

ISABELLE
You spoke with him? What, dressed in this disguise?

ROSALINE
He was rehearsing in the royal ballroom;
I stumbled on him unexpectedly,
While working with the chanteuse, Jaquenetta.

COSTARD
(Aside) Jaquenetta? In the palace? Singing? I must find her at once!

(Exit COSTARD.)

MARIA: Why did you not reveal yourself to him?

ROSALINE
I had intended to reveal myself,
But then I did bethink me: why should I
Remove these pants to satisfy a man?
For look you now, this simple pair of trousers
Hath brought me freedom and equality,
Yea, so much so, that now I am unfit
For petticoat and lace; for when I shed
My woman's clothes, I shed my woman's doubts,
My woman's fears, my woman's servitude,
And nevermore will those harsh garments fit,
So long as I do wear my woman's wit.

ISABELLE
Emmanuel Lanier may say these things,
But Rosaline doth love the Lord Berowne;
And shall Lanier suppress the free election

Of Rosaline's true heart? If so, thou art
Diminish'd by thine own equality,
Enfetter'd by thy long-sought-after freedom;
For though thou hast thrown off thy woman's clothes,
A woman's blood e'en now within thee flows.

ROSALINE
Alas, 'tis true, my loving friends, 'tis true!
I prithee counsel me, what shall I do?

KATHERINE
You must needs show him boldly whom thou art,
And pledge him all the love that's in your heart!

ISABELLE
What's true for Rosaline is true for all;
And therefore must we let our armor fall,
And to our lovers our true love unmask.

MARIA
Then let us each now undertake this task:
Go thou to Ferdinand, to stand up for his cause;
Go thou to Lord Berowne, t'absolve him of his flaws;
Go thou to Lord Dumaine, his ring to give away;
And I to Longaville, to win another day.
I have given you commands.

ROSALINE
I shall not fail.

ISABELLE
          Nor I;

KATHERINE
               Nor I;

MARIA

                    Nor I.

(Exit ALL, separately.)

SCENE 7: THE PALACE BALLROOM

(Enter JAQUENETTA.)

JAQUENETTA *(Singing)*
I once was sure we were forever,
That we would always walk
Together hand in hand,
But as it turned out I was too clever,
And things did not work out
Quite the way I had planned,

So now you're
Gone and my heart is breaking,
Gone and there's no mistaking,
Gone is the love that we shared;

(Enter COSTARD, who stands aside, unseen by JAQUENETTA.)

Gone are the days of gladness,
Gone are the tears of sadness,
The blissful nights, the fits of madness;

Gone are the songs we sang, dear,
Gone are the bells that rang, dear,
For my hopes and dreams
Are all gone.

(COSTARD reveals himself.)

COSTARD
Jaquenetta? Is it you? I do not trust my one good eye, nor my two ears, for many times I've heard your voice, heard you singing sweetly, like an angel in paradise, thinking I was dead, only to find that I was asleep, that I was dreaming, that I was lying in a muddy ditch, covered in blood, with bullets flying at my skull.

JAQUENETTA
Yes, it's me, love; and you are very much alive.

COSTARD
And am I awake?

JAQUENETTA
Yea, thou art awake.

COSTARD
And yet, before me do I see an angel.

JAQUENETTA
A fallen angel, perhaps.

COSTARD
Where is his excellency, Don Adriano de Armado?

JAQUENETTA
Gone. Under enemy fire, he beat a quick retreat, and fled for Spain. He was arrested before he got there.

COSTARD
And what happened to him?

JAQUENETTA
Executed for desertion.

COSTARD
And the baby? Where is your baby?

JAQUENETTA
Gone. Miscarried. The child is dead.

COSTARD
I'm sorry. Very sorry for you.

JAQUENETTA
As am I for you.

COSTARD
I know not what you mean.

JAQUENETTA
The child was not Armado's; 'twas yours.

COSTARD
Mine?

JAQUENETTA
Yours.

COSTARD
But you told me it was his.

JAQUENETTA
That was a lie: 'twas yours.

COSTARD
How dost thou know the child was mine?

JAQUENETTA
Though I may be a liar, the moon is not. I was with child a

week before Armado arrived in the court of Navarre. I told you then that I was two months gone, but I was three.

COSTARD
Can you prove that this is true?

JAQUENETTA
Nay, I cannot. But why should I lie to you now? What have I to gain?

COSTARD
Why didst thou lie to me then?

JAQUENETTA
I hoped the child would do better growing up as the heir of a Spanish nobleman.

COSTARD
But, did not you love Armado?

JAQUENETTA
No. 'Twas never him I loved. 'Twas you. Always you.

COSTARD
And am I now expected to forgive you?

JAQUENETTA
I expect that you'll despise me. But now, at least, I've told the truth. So I can begin to forgive myself.

COSTARD
Stillborn?

JAQUENETTA
Stillborn. As was our love.

COSTARD
I must return before I'm missed.

(Exit COSTARD.)

JAQUENETTA
And here I shall remain, unkissed.

(As JAQUENETTA sings, one by one the lovers appear and cross the stage, just missing one another, searching...)

JAQUENETTA *(Singing)*
And now I walk the path alone, dear;
There's no one by my side,
It seems I've lost my way;
And though I'll try to make it on my own, dear,
How I would give anything
Just to have one more day.

But now you're
Gone and I can't stop crying,
Gone and now there's no denying,
Gone is the lifetime
You promised we'd share;
Gone are the long embraces,
Gone are the tearful faces,
The holding hands, the secret places,

Gone are the days of laughter,
Gone is the ever-after,
For the love of my life
Now has gone.

(Exit JAQUENETTA.)

INTERMISSION

ACT TWO

SCENE 8: A ROOM IN THE PALACE

(Enter DUMAINE, as a distant bell strikes a melody of 16 notes, then the hour of NINE.)

DUMAINE
Another wing? Another corridor?
Another serpentine arcade? *Mort Dieu!*
The devil damn the thimble-witted Costard
For hazarding me thus—and losing me—
In this unnavigable labyrinth!
What? Must a man assemble wings of wax
To fly above the bound'ries of this maze?
By this hath Ferdinand convinced himself
Dumaine's a foul traitor, a deserter,
And therefore shall I hang not once but twice,
Losing my venture with a pair of kings.
And yet not so, for now I do perceive
Iscariot himself, bent on self-destruction,
Could not have given o'er his life within
The bowels of this captivating palace,
For it is so immeasurably immense
That death hath ne'er a prayer of finding thee.
Or else, perchance I am already dead,
And this same palace is a gilded limbo
Where I am doomed to wander ceaselessly
Till I redeem myself for dubious actions
I perpetrated while I was alive.

(Enter KATHERINE.)

I must be dead, for hither comes an angel
That on her back will shepherd me to heaven.

KATHERINE
With whom dost thou converse, my Lord Dumaine?

DUMAINE
I sue to heaven to lead me from despair,
And thou art come: the answer to my prayer.

KATHERINE
No answer, but a question do I bring—

DUMAINE
I long to know thy question, precious thing,
Yet, by your leave, let's talk along the way,
For, by a fool I have been led astray
And now must find my King, if you'll assist,
For that my prudent counsel shall be missed.
Wilt take me there apace?

KATHERINE
                    My question first.

DUMAINE
Have patience, love, for I do fear the worst,
And must insist—

KATHERINE
               I prithee, dost thou love me?

DUMAINE
How can'st thou, Katherine, harbor any doubt,
When for thy love I've borne four years of drought?

KATHERINE
Is this thine answer? Why, a lifeless stone
Can bear four years of drought, or forty years,
Or forty thousand thousand, for it hath
No feeling and will sit unmoved until
The end of time; but thou, a mortal man,
Must prove undying love through worthy action,
For selfless deeds betoken true devotion,
And noble feats do banish ling'ring doubt:
And so it shall prove true if thou lov'st me.

DUMAINE
Then come, bid me do anything for thee.
I would swim oceans, lions brave, eat fire
To grant thy soul whate'er it dost desire:
Like Hannibal, I would the alps traverse,
Like Midas, with a touch I'd gild thy purse,
Like England's George, I'd pierce the dragon's heart,
Like Moses, I'd command the Red Sea part,
Like Menelaus, rescue thee from Troy,
Like Atlas, I would make this globe thy toy.

KATHERINE
I have no need for such celestial deeds,
Accomplishèd by gods and men immortal,
But rather do I crave a modest task
Dischargèd by a kind and gentle man
Who loves me more than he doth love himself:
Wilt know it?

DUMAINE
             Name it, and 'tis done.

KATHERINE
                                    Then thus:
I prithee, take this bauble back again.

DUMAINE
I understand thee not, dear heart. Wherefore?

KATHERINE
For that I'd rather have a hangman's noose
Around my tender neck than this same ring
Upon my finger.

DUMAINE
               Sweet one, if the ring
Doth fail to please thine eye, I shall procure
The finest ring in all of Europe, yea,
The finest necklace, too, and find them out
By proclamation.

KATHERINE
               Nay, the finest jewels
In all the world would fail to please mine eye,
For now my tender heart doth comprehend
The true cost of thy gift, 'tis hateful to me.

DUMAINE
It cost too little, love?

KATHERINE
               It cost too much!
For this bewitching, seeming-spotless ring
Is but the treacherous and deadly offspring
Conceivèd by insatiable, cruel war;
'Tis but the monstrous progeny brought forth
Into the world by avarice and slaughter,
The issue bred of wretchedness and lust,
The child born of suffering and torture;
And therefore, lord, this misbegotten babe
I'll not adopt, nor take unto my bosom,

Nor care for it as if it were mine own.
Here, take it back again.

DUMAINE
                      You speak as if
I were great Mars himself, chief architect
Of man's vast edifice of self-destruction,
And yet, thou know'st I did not start this war,
Nor do I have the pow'r to finish it.

KATHERINE
And yet, I know you profit from this war,
Nor dost thy weaponry diminish it.

DUMAINE
Would'st thou to war send soldiers empty-handed?

KATHERINE
I'd send them home and see their troops disbanded.

DUMAINE
The weapons I supply do France defend.

KATHERINE
You do supply both enemy and friend.

DUMAINE
Both friend and foe alike must arm their sons.

KATHERINE
And both must perish, cut down by your guns.

DUMAINE
Forgive me, Kate, I'll not take back this jewel.

KATHERINE
I see thou dost mistake me for a fool!
Did'st thou not vow to do a noble feat,
And dost thou now for clemency entreat?

DUMAINE
Vouchsafe me then another task to render.

KATHERINE
I will, if to my will you will surrender.

DUMAINE
I place myself into your lenient hands.

KATHERINE
Then hear, good sir, my merciful demands:
If thou would'st have my love and marry me
You must renounce the sale of weaponry.

DUMAINE
What, art thou mad? You ask too much!

KATHERINE
                              There's more:
To stop the bloodshed virtue must abhor,
The arms thou hast in stock thou shalt destroy,
Depriving men of weapons to employ.

DUMAINE
Impossible! Preposterous!

KATHERINE
                    More still:
To rescue those made destitute and ill,
You must bestow your misbegotten wealth
On children who have lost their homes and health.

DUMAINE
I will not do it. Not to be believ'd!

KATHERINE
Alas, my foolish heart is much bereav'd!
Then have I nothing more to say to thee,
Save this: be wedded to thy armory
And loyal husband to thy dear munitions,
And with thine arms embrace thy raw ambitions
And bring forth sons of iron, flint, and fire
And teach them how to reign in thy retire,
And in thy lonely keep shalt thou grow old
With no one by to care for thee but gold.
As for this ring, it shall be rudely tossed;
Now, go thy ways, for evermore be lost!

(KATHERINE throws the ring offstage, and exits in another direction.)

DUMAINE
This change of fortune doth my wit confound!
I'll chase thee, bauble, like an English hound!

(Exit DUMAINE.)

SCENE 9: THE PALACE BALLROOM

(Enter BEROWNE, drinking.)

BEROWNE *(Singing)*
I asked sweet Margaret for her hand,
"First prove thy love," said she,
So I marched off across the land
To prove my chivalry.

When I returned with wedding band,
"Thou'rt come too late," she said,
"For whiles you fought to win my hand,
Dick won it in my bed."

Ha! This is a scurrilous verse to sing at a man's hanging. But here's my comfort!

(Enter ROSALINE, disguised as Lanier.)

ROSALINE *(Aside)*
I heard his voice along this passageway,
And there he is! Alack, what shall I say?
I've built an armor 'round my heart so hard
That it can hardly beat without a guard;
And though this wall doth shield me from life's blows,
It blocks the sunlight where affection grows.
Disguise, though at the start you set me free,
I now perceive thou dost imprison me.
I must reveal myself to him, or rue it;
And yet, poor fool, I know not how to do it!
Then, improvise, till he can plainly see
The naked truth of thy duplicity.

(ROSALINE steps forward.)

How now, brave captain?

BEROWNE
                    Greetings, good Lanier!
I prithee, penman, what's the newest news?

ROSALINE
I've news to share, if thou wilt lend an ear.

BEROWNE
To thee, I'll lend the shirt upon my back,
These trousers, too, if thy new news be good.
Say, is the war over?

ROSALINE
                Nay, no such matter.

BEROWNE
Then is the French King dead?

ROSALINE
                No, 'tis not so.

BEROWNE
Hath Longaville been freed?

ROSALINE
                Hath not, my lord.

BEROWNE
Then I will keep my trousers and my shirt,
For thy new news is old news, old as dirt.

(BEROWNE starts to exit.)

ROSALINE *(Aside)*
My resolution now begins to run
Like icicles that spy the morning sun!
(To BEROWNE) Will you not stay, my friend, to hear the pith?

BEROWNE
I must attend a funeral forthwith,
For in this heat, the body will not last.

ROSALINE
Unhappy tidings; prithee, who hath passed?

BEROWNE
By'r lady, that shall I.

ROSALINE
So shall we all;
But, surely, not today.

BEROWNE
Yea, I shall fall;
The Emperor shall downward point his thumb,
And with a snap my final breath shall come.
Wilt drink a health with me to the departed?

ROSALINE
Begins the wake ere funeral hath started?

BEROWNE
The wake begins the moment we are born.

ROSALINE
The beauty of the rose must have a thorn.

BEROWNE
Nay, if you prick me with your thorn, farewell.

ROSALINE
I have no prick, and that my friends can tell.

BEROWNE
Art thou a friend? Then grant me one request.

ROSALINE
And what is that?

BEROWNE
                When I am laid to rest,
Lanier, wilt thou compose mine epitaph?

ROSALINE
An elegy I'll scribe on thy behalf,
And nightly will I tell it o'er thy shroud:
An epic tale to make great Ovid proud.

BEROWNE
A morsel, come!

ROSALINE
                Yea, marry, for a taste:
"The Captain's charitable works in military hospitals
throughout Europe, cheering the speechless sick, amusing
groaning wretches, and coaxing the painèd impotent to smile,
surely qualify him for commendation as one of the great unsung
heroes of this conflict."

BEROWNE
Dost thou mean to mock me, sirrah inkling? Ovid might call
this monumental theft, for these pretty words of praisement
are not thine.

(He snatches the article from her hands.)

ROSALINE
The praise belongs to thee, the prose is mine.

BEROWNE
How cam'st thou by this artifact, monsieur?

ROSALINE
I had it of thy love.

BEROWNE
     Of Rosaline?

ROSALINE
Yea, even she.

BEROWNE
     And dost thou know her well?

ROSALINE
As well, monsieur, as I do know myself;
Ay, every inch of her.

BEROWNE
     Are you that close?

ROSALINE
Indeed, we are as close as close can be,
That walk about the earth as two, and yet,
Lie down as one.

BEROWNE
     O villainous dissembler!
Thou shalt deny what thou hast said, or I
Shall tear thy truthless tongue out by the root!

ROSALINE
I cannot contradict that which is true,
Which I shall prove if thou wilt give me leave.

BEROWNE
Give thee leave? Why, thou effeminate, snot-nosed ink-blot! I'll give thee leave to prove thyself a coward, thou unwiped lily-

livered villian. Thou broken-quilled, weak-kneed, bony-fingered, puppy-headed paperweight!

ROSALINE
Nay, hear me speak with patience, gentle friend.

BEROWNE
My blows shall stop thy mouth and there an end.

ROSALINE
You know not what you do, Monsieur Berowne.

BEROWNE
I teach thee, youth, to sing another tune.

ROSALINE
Nay, if you seek a fight, I shall not run!

BEROWNE
Stand still, then, sir!

ROSALINE
(Aside) Alack, what have I done?

BEROWNE
Recite thy prayers: thy destiny is grave.

(BEROWNE attempts to throw a punch at ROSALINE.)

ROSALINE
Then gravity my destiny must save.

(ROSALINE knocks BEROWNE to the ground.)

You drunken fool! Dost thou not know me yet?

BEROWNE
Nay, leave my sodden body on the ground;
I have no wish to go another round.

ROSALINE
Arise, I prithee, look upon my face!

BEROWNE
Thy ample manhood thou hast ratified;
Then get you hence, Lanier, be satisfied!

(ROSALINE throws off her hat and coat.)

ROSALINE
I am thy Rosaline! I'm Rosaline, say I!

BEROWNE
Rosaline?

ROSALINE
Am I so changed that thou can'st look upon this face and see no jot of Rosaline?

BEROWNE
What mine eyes do see, my heart will not believe. Art thou my Rosaline?

ROSALINE
Truly, I am she.

BEROWNE
Wast thou Lanier?

ROSALINE
I was, my lord.

BEROWNE
It cannot be.

ROSALINE
And yet, my love, 'tis so.

BEROWNE
Did'st thou, dissembling Lanier, behold me on the stage in Bordeaux?

ROSALINE
I do confess, three years ago, in Bordeaux, surrounded by hostility, I watched thee shake off danger armed with naught but humor and humility.

BEROWNE
You penned the article I sent to thee as proof?

ROSALINE
Every word, my lord.

BEROWNE
And knew that I had faithfully fulfilled my vow?

ROSALINE
To the letter, love.

BEROWNE
Yet you said nothing to me?

ROSALINE
Nothing, my lord, I do confess, 'tis true.

BEROWNE
And all my letters and entreaties, what of them?

ROSALINE
I read them, saved them, kissed them, cherished them, but could not bring myself to answer them.

BEROWNE
Was not this cruel and unjust treatment to inflict upon thy love?

ROSALINE
It was, my lord, I am ashamed to say, it was.

BEROWNE
For this I might shed tears, but that these hollow eyes do not remember how.

ROSALINE
Let mine eyes teach them, for they do water even now.

BEROWNE
Rather, I'll close their rusty gates, banishing sorrow from my sight. And therefore, hence, Lanier, be on your way.

ROSALINE
I shall not go till I have had my say;
For I do stand before your lordship now
As doth a prisoner before a judge
Who doth anticipate a fatal sentence,
Having confess'd a catalogue of crimes
For which the goddess Nemesis herself
Might well devise the sternest punishment,
Yet, nonetheless, doth pray to hear of mercy.
Therefore, my lord, with bottomless remorse,
With true repentance, and with wounding shame,
I beg thy understanding and forgiveness,
Which I do know to be within the compass
Of thy compassionate and noble heart,

For I, who am indeed thy Rosaline,
Do solemnly declare before my judge,
In spite of my lamentable transgressions,
That I do love you dearly and eternally,
And if thy love for me doth persevere
As ardently as once thou did'st profess,
I'll take thy hand, as years ago I swore,
And be thy faithful wife for evermore.

BEROWNE
I'm sorry to report, but 'tis my duty,
My love for thee is dead, it's buried, gone;
It perish'd on the savage battlefield,
Where, wounded fatally and losing blood,
It lay down in a trench, and comfortless,
Forgotten, cold, alone, it left this world,
With only bitterness and anger by
To mourn the pitiless and sad depart.

ROSALINE
Alack, this elegy doth break my heart.
Is there no remedy? No hope?

BEROWNE
                    There's none.

ROSALINE
And wilt thou not forgive?

BEROWNE
                    No. Never. Done.

(Exit BEROWNE.)

ROSALINE
Alack! Methinks I am too cruel to live!

And yet, how cruel is he to not forgive!
I shall seek out some quiet place to weep,
For that which I have sown, now do I reap.

(ROSALINE picks up her hat and coat, and exits.)

SCENE 10: ANOTHER ROOM IN THE PALACE

(Enter FERDINAND and ISABELLE.)

ISABELLE
I understand you not: you took an oath?

FERDINAND
We three did swear, swear boldly, by my troth,
To stake our lives against the King's decree.

ISABELLE
But wherefore to this pledge would you agree?
What certain benefit is to be gained
By hazarding your lives? What good obtained?

FERDINAND
The certain good that we adventur'd all,
Befall the harshest fate that might befall,
In our attempt to liberate a friend.

ISABELLE
Beshrew me, I shall never comprehend,
Live I a hundred years, what demon 'tis
Drives men to make such reckless promises.

FERDINAND
That demon's name is honor, and divine
When brothers band together, as do mine.

ISABELLE
Your band will be arrested by the guard,
And every hope of rescue shall be marred.

FERDINAND
Then show me where Lord Longaville is hidden.

ISABELLE
I cannot; I expressly am forbidden
And must abide the judgement of my brother.

FERDINAND
No Solomon is he, abide some other.

ISABELLE
A king should know, if he knows anything,
Obey I must the dictates of a king.

FERDINAND
The dictates of a king, the world take note,
Would place a noose around a guiltless throat!

ISABELLE
Thou dost offend when thou dost malice pour
Upon the son my father did adore!

FERDINAND
Thou dost offend to let thy father's son
Undo the good thy father would have done!

(A pause.)

ISABELLE
Dost thou remember him, my lord?

FERDINAND
                                 I do.
He was the noblest man that e'er I knew.
In sooth, I wish that he were still alive.

ISABELLE
How I do wish thy wish could him revive.
Dost thou recall the day we heard the news?

FERDINAND
Remembrance of that day I ne'er shall lose:
His unexpected death our hopes did dash.

ISABELLE
And turned the fields of Europe into ash.

FERDINAND
O how my soul would heartily rejoice
To hear the sound of his resounding voice
Recounting tales of his adventurous youth.

ISABELLE
To see the glimmer in his eyes! Forsooth,
I feel his boundless loss, though four years past,
As doth a ship adrift without a mast.

FERDINAND
No finer man did stride the earth than he.

ISABELLE
My lord, my father often spoke of thee,
Praising thy virtue and thy worthiness,

And 'twas his fervent hope, I must confess,
To see the day your grace and I might wed.

FERDINAND
I did suspect as much, for that he fed
My hungry ear, when last I saw his face,
With soaring commendations of thy grace,
Thy modesty, and most of all, thy beauty.

ISABELLE
Why then, in keeping with a daughter's duty,
I beg your patient leave that I may speak
More boldly than I otherwise might seek.

FERDINAND
For his sake, I attend thy will.

ISABELLE
                     Then this:
I pray you, sign the present armistice.

FERDINAND
My country and my crown shall I betray?

ISABELLE
'Twill not be so, for I do spy a way
To honor my dear father's will
And save the life of Longaville,
If thou wilt entertain what I propose.

FERDINAND
What way is that? Thy strategem disclose.

(ISABELLE kneels.)

ISABELLE
In Notre Dame Cathedral take my hand,
And make a solemn oath, upon thy life,
As merry bells do chime throughout the land,
To love me as thy true and faithful wife.

FERDINAND
A bold and most surprising proposition!
But how doth this my royalty maintain?
For once I put my name to this submission,
The end of war will also end my reign.

ISABELLE
You would not henceforth be a reigning king,
But o'er the realm of France a royal prince,
And we shall set aright the suffering
We've seen across the land these four years since.

FERDINAND
The logic of your reasoning doth jar:
For marriage may a resolution bring,
But how doth this alliance save Navarre?

ISABELLE
Once married, I'll impress upon the King,
Thy newly-minted brother, to present,
That he might heal this continental rift,
Navarre to us as royal testament,
Bestowing peace as our true wedding gift.

FERDINAND
Thou dost importune me to abdicate
All dignity and honor to my foe!

ISABELLE
I do importune thee to set aside
Thy royal pride to forstall further woe.

FERDINAND
If you did love me, you would rather ask,
For honor's sake, that I lay down my life.

ISABELLE
If you did love me, you would give consent,
For honor's sake, to make me thy dear wife.

FERDINAND
To do so, I should lose the present war
And live a life of everlasting shame.

ISABELLE
To do so, you should win a present peace
And conquer death through everlasting fame.

FERDINAND
It cannot be, the stain shall be too great!

ISABELLE
Yet must it be, for Longaville can't wait!

FERDINAND
I'll find my men myself, and soldier on!

(Exit FERDINAND.)

ISABELLE
And I my women, for now my hopes are gone!

(Exit ISABELLE, in another direction.)

SCENE II: THE PALACE DUNGEON

(We hear a heavy steel door being slammed and locked.)

(Enter MARIA and DUMAINE.)

DUMAINE
I do not like this place, it stinks of death.

MARIA
Nay, come along, my lord, you need not fear;
No injury shall come to you down here;
I'll be your escort and your surety.

DUMAINE
Nay, art thou certain? For this passage seems
The dank and slipp'ry way to Hades' gate.
Dost thou not, Virgil-like, conduct me to
The dreary banks whereon the hellish boatman
Charon awaits to pilot downcast souls
Across the river Styx, where they must face,
For wickedness they did commit above,
The torments of the King of fiery hell?

MARIA
Do not abandon hope in this deep place;
I do assure you here no demons dwell,
But only bashful rats and spineless spiders
That eagerly will flee the sight of us,
Stockpiles of wine aging without complaint,
Twelve centuries of books sequestered still,
And gems too rare to live among the living:
Les Diamants de la Couronne de France.

DUMAINE
O, pardon mon français, what was the last?

MARIA
The French Crown Jewels, that last did leave these vaults
When Louis, as a youth, was crownèd sovereign.

DUMAINE
The scepters, brooches, diadems and orbs
That dress the royal stage of coronation
Reside in this dark place?

MARIA
                They are entomb'd
Where they were born, so peerless-precious that
The bowels of this dismal world must house them.

DUMAINE
Sleep they nearby, Maria? Might we rouse them?

MARIA
I know not where they're guarded 'neath the earth.

DUMAINE
Then are they pris'ners of their own dear worth.
Well, 'tis no matter, for I do perceive,
What though a man may stamp or fret or grieve,
He cannot buy the most desired thing
Though he possess the ransom of a king.

MARIA
I understand thee not, Monsieur Dumaine.

DUMAINE
I think thou dost, *mamzel*, I think thou dost.

MARIA
Yet, here's a treasure of another sort
That hath, to me, inestimable value.

DUMAINE
What treasure's that?

LONGAVILLE
          Who goes there?

MARIA
                    'Tis a friend.

(LONGAVILLE appears.)

I've brought a visitor, Lord Longaville.

LONGAVILLE
Welcome, Dumaine, unto to my humble cell!
Four trips around the sun have served you well.
Nay, come, I prithee, there's no need to fear,
You'll find no danger nor no torture here.

(LONGAVILLE embraces DUMAINE, as MARIA exits.)

DUMAINE
Art thou our long-lost Longaville indeed?
Thou art a fraction of the man thou wast.

LONGAVILLE
That I am less in flesh 'tis true, but then,
In spirit have I grown immeasurably.

DUMAINE
Do they attempt to execute thee, friend,
By starving thee one morsel at a time?

LONGAVILLE
Nay, to the contrary, my gracious captors
Have fed me well, for they have furnish'd me
With life-sustaining books, which I've consum'd
Most greedily, a never-ending feast
Of all the human knowledge ever penn'd.

DUMAINE
I've known the kind of man who eats his words,
But thou dost take the diet to extremes!

(Enter MARIA with BEROWNE.)

BEROWNE *(Singing)*
I asked,"Where doth a man
Find some love in this town?
I've fought with my wife
And I'm in great distress."

The tapster just smiled
As he wrote something down,
And he winked as he handed me
Mine own address!

MARIA
Nay, captain, take my arm lest you should fall.

BEROWNE
I thank thee for this kindness, ossifer,
But there's no need to molly-coddle me!
These feet well know the way to ambulate
The one behind the one before the other.

MARIA
I'm loath to see thee kiss these stones, monsieur,
For thou shalt find them hard and unforgiving.

BEROWNE
As woman's love? Ha! Fear you not, good sir!
I came upon them in another chamber,
And now my ardor for them hath been spent.
Is this the cellar where the King doth keep
His wine? 'Tis well, for I am passing empty.

LONGAVILLE
My Lord Berowne! Let me embrace thee, friend!

BEROWNE
I prithee, do not jostle me about;
My stomach is a most unfaithful wretch.

LONGAVILLE
Come, make yourself a place within my home;
For all that I call mine is ever thine.

(Exit MARIA.)

BEROWNE
Art thou the vintner? Then uncork me here
A bottle of the sovereign's finest vintage!
I'll taste the sweetness of his hospitality
Before I swallow down the dregs of his injustice.

DUMAINE
Hast thou not whined enough already, cap?

BEROWNE
Monsieur Dumaine! I relish this good hap!
Wilt drain a bottle with me? Say not nay!
Two bottles, sirrah, bring us, straightaway!

LONGAVILLE
Wilt thou drink honest water, good Berowne?
For that is all I have to offer thee.

BEROWNE
What say'st thou, sirrah? Water, villain? Pish!
Dost thou mistake me for a finless fish?

DUMAINE
He doth mistake thee for a drowning man.

BEROWNE
Not so! I swim as well as any mortal can.

DUMAINE
'Tis true, for thou dost swim in thine own pity.

BEROWNE
And thou dost sink in straining to be witty.

DUMAINE
I strain myself in training up a mule.
Dost thou not recognize this man, you fool?

BEROWNE
His hollow face I seem to recognize.
Art thou the hangman come to claim thy prize?

DUMAINE
Why this is Longaville, you witless sponge!

BEROWNE
Is't so? Lord Longaville? How joy doth woe expunge!
Belovèd sir, how I have miss'd thy face!

(BEROWNE embraces LONGAVILLE, lifting and spinning him.)

LONGAVILLE
As I have miss'd thy boisterous embrace.

(Enter MARIA with FERDINAND.)

FERDINAND
Will not the King severely chastise thee
For bringing me where Longaville is held?

MARIA
Let me assure your grace, in showing thee
The aspects of the palace lesser known,
Well hidden from the view of common eyes,
I do extend a royal courtesy
The likes of which the King himself, with pride,
Might show thee as a merriment, not hide.

FERDINAND
In thee, Maria, France is surely bless'd,
Whose wisdom sees a way to do what's best.

LONGAVILLE
My lord, let me embrace thy royal frame.

FERDINAND
Art thou our Longaville?

LONGAVILLE
                              My liege, the same.

FERDINAND
Did not I recognize thy golden tones,
I tell thee, with a ghost I might be frighten'd.

LONGAVILLE
'Tis true, the burden on these flimsy bones
By time hath been considerably lighten'd.

(FERDINAND embraces LONGAVILLE.)

FERDINAND
Behold, we four, though four years gone astray,
By answering proud honor's loud alarms,
Do fortify our friendship on this day:
Stand proudly then, affection's men-at-arms!

BEROWNE
Think'st thou we are affection's warriors?
Or are we not her abject prisoners?
Captured for stealing her quiver and bow
And thrust in her dungeon to quiver below.

LONGAVILLE
I see no pris'ners here, my Lord Berowne,
But free, undaunted men, whose ardent hearts
Cannot be bound within the stony limits
Of these, or any, barricades or walls;
For where love dwells, no barriers can be;
So love doth free us unconditionally.

FERDINAND
My noble lord, thou dost astonish me!
For I did think to find you suffering
Beyond the bounds of man's capacity.
How hast thou come by such profound contentment
Within the confines of this dismal cell?

LONGAVILLE
I'll gladly share the way I've persever'd
If thou wilt stay to hear what I shall tell.

FERDINAND
Yea, truly shall we.

DUMAINE
　　Let us hear thee speak.

LONGAVILLE
Then, sit, my friends. Although this cell doth lack
Good furniture, this earth shall well support us.
Prithee, sit.

(They sit upon the ground.)

MARIA
(Aside) Successfully I've mustered up these four;
Once more then overhead to find one more!

(Exit MARIA.)

FERDINAND
Now tell us truly: how hast thou surviv'd
And thriv'd in these draconian conditions?

LONGAVILLE
At first, when I was placèd in this cell,
Without possessions, comfort, friendship, hope,
I fell into an ocean of despair
Wherein, no will to swim, I nearly drown'd.

DUMAINE
But how did'st thou shake off this deep despair?

LONGAVILLE
It was the thought of all of you, my friends,
That freed me from the grip of melancholy,
For in a quiet moment of reflection

I did remember how, before this war,
To trumpet our ambitious fellowship
Upon the drowsy eardrums of the world,
We made a solemn vow to one another
To disallow the company of women,
To fast, to study, and to forgo sleep.

FERDINAND
We do remember well these brazen vows.

LONGAVILLE
Then well you will remember, too, my liege,
These oaths we found impossible to keep
Against the raging currents of our blood
And the voracious cravings of our youth.

FERDINAND
How innocent our lives before the war!

DUMAINE
How carefree and how frivolous!

BEROWNE
How celibate and sober!

FERDINAND
Go on, my noble lord: what happened next?

LONGAVILLE
In that same moment, friends, bethinking this,
My tortured soul did wholly comprehend:
To tolerate my present circumstance
I must perforce renew those broken vows
That none of us could heed in greener days.

FERDINAND
But how did this awareness put an end
To thy distress?

LONGAVILLE
          Those first long months, it could not;
And yet, I slowly came to recognize
That my confinement in this tiny cell,
Depriving me of every thing I cherish'd,
Of all that I believ'd sustained my life,
Provided me with something far more precious:
A rich supply of time to meditate
Upon my fleeting presence on this earth,
Through which, with the assistance of my books
And good Maria's gentle loving care,
I have awaken'd to contentment far beyond
The bounds of what I e'er imagin'd possible.

DUMAINE
How canst thou, having nothing, be content?

LONGAVILLE
I am content for I desire nothing.

BEROWNE
Desire nothing? How can this be so?

LONGAVILLE
After a thousand turnings of the earth,
With rumination and privation as
My faithful tutors, I did come to see
That seeking to possess great wealth
Had been the root of my unhappiness;
That my ambition, which did elbow me
To strive for higher-still accomplishment,
Would ne'er be satisfied; that vanity,

Which spurr'd me on to quest for greater fame,
Would ne'er be quiet; so it was I came
To understand that craving not—not owning,
Not striving, not desiring—was the way
To end my constant suffering, the way
To peace and happiness.

BEROWNE
                    I am amaz'd.
Is't possible that thou canst feel no anger?
No bitterness towards those that injured you?
No appetite to seek a sweet revenge?

LONGAVILLE
When I did come unto this lonesome cell,
My anger for my captors was my all:
I ate my anger, drank my anger, breath'd
My anger, spew'd my anger, bled my anger;
But over time I've come to understand
That anger is a most pernicious poison
For which forgiveness is the only cure.

FERDINAND
Yet, how canst thou abide this loss of power?
How brook the insult to thy dignity?
How pardon those that would not pardon thee?

LONGAVILLE
Through contemplation I have seen
That joy and peace are never to be found
Until you're willing to embrace each loss,
Until you're willing to let go of blame,
Until you're willing to accept what is.
For look at me, deprived of everything,
And yet more joyful and content with life
Than any of you three, who strive for wealth,

Hunger for power, thirst for eminence,
Who carry bitterness and anger like
A soldier's blunted sword and batter'd shield,
Whose minds do dwell in shadows of the past,
Or brood upon bright musings of the future,
But rarely stand awaken'd to the present:
Delusions that do still perpetuate
The discontent which you yourselves have made.

BEROWNE
Yet, what is to be done? For we are made
Of flesh and blood; not holy saints, nor gods,
But mortal men, with appetites and passions!

LONGAVILLE
'Tis not for me to say, for each of you,
Through contemplation of your own delusions,
Must answer that same question for yourselves.

(Enter MARIA with COSTARD.)

MARIA
Can this majestic chamber hold one more?
For here's another wayward visitor!

LONGAVILLE
Good Costard, welcome!

COSTARD
Lord Longaville?

(COSTARD and LONGAVILLE embrace.)

FERDINAND
Where hast thou been, Corporal?

COSTARD
Where have I been? Nay, where are you? I thought you were forever lost at sea. For there I was, ruddering my vessel through narrow straits, when the singing of the Sirens lured my seamen to the rocks. As for me, if Maria had not tugged upon my hull, I had been swallowed whole within the swirling mouth of Charybdis.

MARIA
Indeed, I found him prowling the palace as a mouse for cheese. Hast thou not news to share, good Corporal? Say.

COSTARD
Corporal Say? I am not Corporal Say! Corporal Say is dead, mistress, he's gone: his throat slit open by Lieutenant Do.

DUMAINE
Slit open? Do you mean to say that Do hath executed Say?

COSTARD
To say the least.

DUMAINE
Wherefore would Do do such a thing to Say as this you say?

COSTARD
Do wouldn't say. But they do say it was for treason.

DUMAINE
Was Say a traitor?

COSTARD
He was, methinks, for that this Say would never do what he told Do that he would do.

DUMAINE
Nay, that won't do.

COSTARD
Indeed, he had the final Say.

DUMAINE
Who did?

COSTARD
Do did. Say had no children, which means that Do undid the final Say.

DUMAINE
I would say 'tis tragic, but to do so would not do Say justice.

COSTARD
Then let us say a prayer for Say.

DUMAINE
I say amen to that.

COSTARD
And so say I; but what do we do about Do?

DUMAINE
Say nothing, or we shall be undone.

COSTARD
I'll do as you say, but 'twill be easier to say than to do.

DUMAINE
When all is said and done, methinks you do say true.

FERDINAND
I say no more of this ado! Thy news, man, thy news!

COSTARD
News? What news? O, the news! My lords, in rooms above they

aim to take a final vote upon the armistice, and you, good King,
are sought in every open bed and unmade closet to face them at
the quill, table in hand.

FERDINAND
Then lead the way, good Corporal.

MARIA
                              Nay, not so!
I prithee, let a woman lead you thither,
For I do know the most straightforward way
To shepherd you to lasting peace today.

BEROWNE
Then let us go.

FERDINAND
           We willingly obey.

(With MARIA leading, FERDINAND, BEROWNE, DUMAINE, and COSTARD each take a brief moment to connect with LONGAVILLE before exiting.)

SCENE 12: THE PALACE GARDENS

(Enter ISABELLE, ROSALINE, and KATHERINE.)

ROSALINE
'Tis almost dawn!

KATHERINE
               Yea, look: the sun doth rise!

ISABELLE
They've battled o'er the peace throughout the night.

KATHERINE
Why should it take so long to compromise?

ROSALINE
Behind closed doors, it's hard to see the light.

KATHERINE
King Ferdinand, perhaps, refused to sign.

ISABELLE
King Louis would not Longaville dare slay.

ROSALINE
I would such certainty as that were mine.

KATHERINE
Where is Maria?

ISABELLE
    Lo, she comes this way!

(Enter MARIA, carrying a copy of the armistice.)

ROSALINE
How now, Maria?

KATHERINE
    Tell us what you know!

ISABELLE
What tidings from the conference of Kings?

MARIA
To speak these news my lungs shall overflow,
My heart's so full of wondrous happenings!

KATHERINE
Then carry not the burden all alone!

MARIA
This day shall generations yet unknown
Remember as the day the peace was signed.

ROSALINE
O happy day!

KATHERINE
    O blessèd, blessèd day!

ISABELLE
A day that monuments shall hence record!

ROSALINE
But share with us the terms of the accord.

MARIA
When that the hour of the clock hath striken one
Four years of bloody conflict shall be done;
The generals shall execute their orders
To march their troops behind their separate borders;
All havoc and disorder shall be ceased,
All prisoners of war shall be released.

ISABELLE
Including Longaville?

KATHERINE
    Dost know his fate?

MARIA
King Louis did at last capitulate:
Within this hour shall Longaville be freed.

ROSALINE
O blissful hour!

KATHERINE
          A joyous day indeed!

ISABELLE
But tell me, what will happen to Navarre?

KATHERINE
And to the factories of Lord Dumaine?

ROSALINE
What of Berowne? Did he the meeting mar?

ISABELLE
And when shall we behold them once again?

MARIA
The three of them shall answer thine appeals;
For they do follow closely on my heels.

(Enter FERDINAND, DUMAINE, and BEROWNE.)

FERDINAND
The King's a beggar.

ISABELLE
          Prithee, say not so.

FERDINAND
I do but speak what all the world shall know:

My kingdom now is but this lump of clay;
For with a pen I signed a realm away;
And therefore, here upon a humble knee,
That knows the way to bend a stubborn leg,
In earnest hope that you shall pardon me,
I'll do as every beggar does: I'll beg.

ISABELLE
I prithee, rise, my lord, you must not plead
For my forgiveness; nay, thou hast no need:
I gave it thee before thou didst entreat.
Your hand, then; stand upon thy noble feet;
For Isabelle's affections, truly told,
Do not depend upon a hoop of gold,
Nor land, nor wealth, nor sacrament, nor sway,
But I shall treasure thee, unfold what may,
And thou shalt be enthronèd in my heart,
Though not upon the throne of France,
And from this day we'll never be apart
To face this life's uncertain circumstance.

FERDINAND
As loving wife and husband, then, let's stand,
And face this life together, hand in hand.

DUMAINE
'Tis my turn, Katherine, to make amends,
For my ambition now hath just one aim:
That from this solitary hell I might,
Like Orpheus, my heavy steps retrace,
To find my way back to thy loving grace.

KATHERINE
Am I Eurydice? Then look not back,
But lead us forward, forward to the light,
Lest I forever vanish from thy sight.

DUMAINE
Nay, never back, dear Kate, but ever forward,
(For thou dost know I'm nothing if not forward);
And to that end, to verify my love
Beyond all doubt, I have, by sign'd agreement,
In solemn ceremony duly seal'd
In sight of heaven's ever-present eye,
Renounc'd the sale of mortal weaponry.

KATHERINE
In plainest terms: pray, tell me what thou mean'st.

DUMAINE
The arms I have in stock shall be destroy'd,
My factories pulled level to the ground,
And nevermore shall be in war deploy'd,
And nevermore shall be in service found.

KATHERINE
Is't even so? Hast done this selfless deed?

DUMAINE
I have, my love; and further have decreed
That all the wealth I earned abetting strife,
And all the profits gained through loss of life,
To hospitals and schools I'll give away
To heal the wounds inflicted by this fray.

KATHERINE
I know not how my rapture to express!

DUMAINE
Then say thou wilt our sacred union bless.

KATHERINE
With all my heart; and much it joys me too
To see thou hast reform'd thyself anew.

ROSALINE
And what of me, my love? and what of me?
Am I condemn'd to be a sorry exile
From thy affection? Or shall I receive
A full and outright pardon for my crimes
Against thy batter'd and abusèd state?

BEROWNE
O gentle Rosaline, what shall I say?
Shall I stand all aloof and be thy judge?
Shall I be jury? Executioner?
Then do I pity thee, poor lady mine,
With all my heart, for if you choose to love
So desolate a man as he that stands
Before you now, truly, thou art condemn'd,
Yea, doomed to live a life of ceaseless woe
If thou would'st yoke thy destiny unto
A bitter, sullen, weary, broken man
Disfigured by the cruelties of war;
A drunken rogue, who desperately did seek
To wound the heart that most he sought to win;
A stubborn wretch, who rudely did refuse,
To her he loves above this world, forgiveness.
Alas, I grieve for thee, sweet Rosaline,
For loving, past all reason, such a man,
And sorely wish that I could offer thee,
From such agregious punishment, reprieve;
And yet, I see in those beguiling eyes,
Thou shalt pursue thy passionate appeal
A mile beyond the precipice of peril;
And therefore—you that witness, mark me well—
I hereby sentence you, most gracious lady,

To marry instantly this same Berowne,
And love him as he is, with all his flaws,
And stand beside him, morning, night, and noon,
And set aside all thoughts of sorrow's cause.

ROSALINE
With all my heart, I do accept my fate,
And I shall love thee with the faults thou hast,
And stand beside thee forward from this date,
And all our trials shall fade into the past.
Then let my punishment commence with this:
By tendering the judge a loving kiss!

(Enter COSTARD, pushing LONGAVILLE in a wheelchair.)

COSTARD
Here is the place, my lord! Did not I say?

LONGAVILLE
I never doubted, friend, you'd find the way.

DUMAINE
Behold! Poor Jonah spit forth from the whale
To drench astonish'd hearers with his tale!

LONGAVILLE
No man is more astonishèd than I,
That joys to see the beauty of the sky.

MARIA
No sight can be more beautiful than this:
To see my love emerge from the abyss.

LONGAVILLE
I am most grateful to thee, friends, for this reprieve.

DUMAINE
We were not ready for thee, friend, to take thy leave!

LONGAVILLE
Thou speak'st aright, the readiness is all;
And yet, to see this peace, I'm pleased withal.

FERDINAND
Maria, most of all, did steer events.

DUMAINE
Though none of us suspected her intents!

MARIA
I merely did what needed to be done.

FERDINAND
By doing so thou hast the war undone.

LONGAVILLE
Is't true, my love? didst thou so intervene?

MARIA
'Tis true, my love, I served as go-between;
I could not let things run their natural course.

BEROWNE
And let the kings of Europe all grow hoarse?

LONGAVILLE
Did I not ask thee, love, to let things be?

MARIA
You did, my love; wilt thou not pardon me?

LONGAVILLE
I shall forgive thee, love; in sooth, I do,
And till the day I die will love thee true.

MARIA
And all my love to thee I do intend,
Until the vasty universe doth end.

FERDINAND
Long live our gentle guide and fearless friend!

DUMAINE
Who teaches us to love and to forgive.

BEROWNE
Who hath enlighten'd us on how to live!

(Enter JAQUENETTA, who embraces BEROWNE.)

JAQUENETTA
Well met, my Captain! I have been sent to seek you out! Where hast thou been?

BEROWNE
In truth, good Jaq, I cannot tell you where I've been, for like a moonless night upon a desert sand, 'tis dark. *(To ROSALINE)* But I can tell you at the present, I am here.

(JAQUENETTA and ROSALINE nod warmly to one another in mutual acceptance.)

JAQUENETTA
Hast heard the joyous news?

BEROWNE
I have.

JAQUENETTA
And is it true?

BEROWNE
It must be true, for I myself did witness the embracements all around.

JAQUENETTA
Then urgently you're needed, Cap. For our evening's entertainment is now a celebration! The European nations have at long last made a peace!

COSTARD
And I, at last, shall make a peace with thee, my lovely Jaquenetta! For these gracious couplings have taught me what is what: that war is war, and peace is peace, and love is love, and forgiveness is the king of all! And therefore, sweet Jaquenetta, dear Jaquenetta, fair Jaquenetta, with all my heart I do forgive you, as I do hope that you will pardon me.

JAQUENETTA
O, my gentle Costard: pardon thee for what?

COSTARD
For any indiscretions that I've done
That I do not remember having done!

JAQUENETTA
I do. With all my heart, I do. And henceforth I shall pledge my faith to you.

COSTARD
And I to thee. And I shall take thee in my arms and call thee wife.

JAQUENETTA
And I shall call thee husband.

COSTARD
And if the fates be kind, this night we'll make a son!

JAQUENETTA
A daughter, too, and if I have my wish!

COSTARD
Thou shalt have two of each, or in thy arms I'll die in the attempt!

ISABELLE
Is't possible that war hath been expelled,
And harmony prevails throughout the land?

BEROWNE
'Tis difficult at present to believe.

KATHERINE
Maria, read the armistice to us,
So that our batter'd, disbelieving hearts
May truly comprehend what hath befallen.

DUMAINE
Yea, read the text aloud so all may hear.

MARIA *(Reads)*
We, the undersigned, hereby declare
A treaty to which we all solemnly swear
Betokens an end to our present calamity,
And the instant commencement of mutual amity,
Of peace everlasting 'mong neighboring nations
Made to advantage unborn generations
That shall not be sundered by uncivil actions,

Nor blighted by rude and self-serving infractions,
But banishes hence all repulsive contending
To outlast the trials of time never-ending.

FERDINAND
An admirable and worthy declaration!

ISABELLE
A blessing to be shared by every nation!

DUMAINE
A cause for unrelenting jubilation!

BEROWNE
My dearest Jaq, our revels have begun!
A song to celebrate that war is done!

ROSALINE
A song to celebrate love's labors won!

(JAQUENETTA moves freely about the room, blessing each of the couples, as well as COSTARD, as she sings.)

JAQUENETTA *(Singing)*
*Now there's no going back
To the time that we lost,
No looking back
To add up the cost,*

*The tears that we shed,
The years that were wasted
Are all behind us;*

*No, there's no going back
To newly begin,*

No looking back
To what might have been,

The roads never tread,
The joys never tasted
Will only blind us;

So let's all agree
To cherish the now,
Lift up our voices
To sing in a vow

We'll walk down the path
Hand-in-hand, day-by-day,
Our love for each other
Will show us the way,

For the tears that we shed
And the years that were wasted
Are all behind us,

Love will show us the way
There's no going back;
Love will show us the way,
There's no going back;
Love will show us the way,
There's no going back.

(*The lovers applaud* JAQUENETTA *as she takes a bow. Overlapping, we hear a bell strike a melody of sixteen notes in the distance, then, after a brief pause, the hour of* ONE. *For a sublime, suspended moment, everyone listens intently to the chime's reverberation—motionless, breathing deeply, feeling profound joy.*)

LONGAVILLE
'Tis one.

(LONGAVILLE dies peacefully in the arms of MARIA.)

(The cast remains motionless, grieving silently.)

(ROSALINE steps forward.)

ROSALINE
Although our play hath found a natural end,
Another story doth remain unpenn'd,
A tale without a curtain call or bow,
A narrative you're writing even now;
So one more gentle word before we part
Which we do offer truly from the heart:
Though life's a thorny path, do not despair,
Nor spend thy precious minutes vexed with care,
But rather keep exploring, inch by inch,
And though the briars scratch thee, do not flinch,
For all our stories come to one conclusion:
We suffer till we give up our delusion.
Let kindness, therefore, be our guide each day
In everything we do and think and say,
Beginning now, when you forgive our flaws,
And offer up your hands in warm applause.

END OF PLAY

ALSO BY SCOTT KAISER

SHAKESPEARE'S OTHER WOMEN:
A NEW ANTHOLOGY OF MONOLOGUES

SPLITTIN' THE RAFT

THE TAO OF SHAKESPEARE

SHAKESPEARE'S WORDCRAFT

MASTERING SHAKESPEARE:
AN ACTING CLASS IN SEVEN SCENES

CPSIA information can be obtained
at www.ICGtesting.com
Printed in the USA
FSHW022009140619
59100FS